DEFY
THE
DARKNESS

A Story of Suicide, Mental Health, and
Overcoming Your Hardest Battles

By

DYLAN J. SESSLER

INVICTUS
DEVELOPMENT GROUP LLC

Print ISBN: 978-1-7372861-0-3
Ebook ISBN: 978-1-7372861-1-0
Library of Congress Control Number: 2021912373

First Edition

For any information regarding collaborating with the author, please contact: Invictus.dev.grp@gmail.com

Visit the author's website at www.DylanSessler.com

Printed in the U.S.A.

This book is typeset in Open Sans and Garamond.

Self-Published by Dylan J. Sessler (www.DylanSessler.com).

From the author: I am not a Mental Health Professional. The thoughts and ideas expressed in this book are based upon my own experiences and my own research. This book will not cure your mental health issues, it will only offer you a different perspective. Understand that your life is different from mine and I assume no liability for losses or damages due to the information provided. Ultimately, you are responsible for your own choices, actions, and results. Finally, if you are struggling with any kind of mental health emergency, please contact the National Suicide Prevention Lifeline: 1-800-273-8255.

Dedicated to the man that showed me how to live.
Rest in Peace
~Donald J. Sessler~
July 17, 1960 – August 12, 1996

CONTENTS

INTRODUCTION

As I watched my father's face, I recognized a dark truth. He wasn't coming back. How could I understand at six years old that he was lying to me for the last time? I don't know how; I just knew there was something profoundly wrong. I felt his pain and suffering through his façade. What I recognized at six years old was a feeling that has yet to be explained outside of "an instinct." My "instincts" were absolutely right. My father left that day and never came home. He ended his life in a secluded park outside my hometown. The dark feeling in the pit of my stomach told me something was wrong before it even happened. What do you do when you are faced with that for the first time in your life? What do you do when you face it as a kid who knows nothing of the world? My ignorance didn't save me from what happened. In fact, it was my ignorance that drove me to the self-destructive decision to put a gun to my own head at age twenty-five because of what I had seen.

What people don't tell you about dealing with suicide or most mental health issues is that it's more than just the blame you place on yourself. It's the darkness you surround yourself with. It's the feelings that remind you of how you and all the people in their life failed to keep them going. In response to what you faced; you vow to make a difference. Although, you forget about yourself in the process because you feel undeserving. They don't tell you about the downward spiral of how guilt compounds your shame and shame compounds your guilt. The onset of the depression, the anxiety, the PTSD just reminds you how lonely you feel, but you believe so deeply that you deserve it for failing them, you remain silent . . . no one would understand anyway. They don't tell you that. They tell you, "it wasn't your fault," like that is supposed to change it all.

There is a sense of animosity when people tell you how to feel when it doesn't feel right. That animosity only isolates and confuses those who struggle even more. *Defy the Darkness* is for anyone who doesn't know how to keep going. It is for the person who is struggling to see beyond their darkest days. It is for all the times someone told you that you aren't good enough. It is for all the life moments that broke you. It is for the people who have been told how they should feel rather than being allowed to feel. It is for all the years you've struggled alone with pain and suffering. It is for every time you've hit rock bottom. I hope that, with this book, you will find a way to step into the light. This book is for you.

If you are struggling to find your purpose or understand the world around you, I am hopeful that *Defy the Darkness* will help you find a way to move forward and step into the light. I have experienced, observed, and carefully studied the effects that life has on people. I didn't get the luxury of living a normal childhood which also gave me the opportunity to pay attention to the world around me. Now, one of the greatest joys in my life is watching people defy the darkness within themselves and learn to truly live. I want this book to serve as your gateway to the life you deserve.

I believe in the power of adaptation and our inherent ability to control human physiology. I believe the human mind is the source of our undeniable power to succeed. Let this book serve as a guiding light to redefining your life. Let it serve as the permission to feel what you need to feel and to love yourself. Allow it to show you how to love your story and value every success and failure you have ever experienced. They have all brought you here to reading this book. Whether this is the worst time of your life, or the best, or somewhere in between, let *Defy the Darkness* remind you that your empathy should also be practiced on yourself first. You can't expect someone else to change a part of you that you should be changing yourself. It will always be up to you.

Many years ago, I found myself searching for a solution to an unanswerable question. It was a simple question, yet one responsible for lasting repercussions in my life. You see, our internal choices affect us the most. Defining who we are as a person requires years, if not decades, of thought and contemplation, and we often don't get it right the first time. In the aftermath of my father's death, I was trying desperately to answer: "Why?" This impossible question caused me to suffer deeply, and time offers no respite from life's many complexities. Even if we try to hide from it, we are always tuned into who we are. The body knows more than we give it credit for; the questions you hide from are the ones that unleash torrents of stress.

My story could have held me underwater my entire life. Every unfortunate thing that happened to me could have served as the fuel for me to continue to play victim. I easily could have resigned myself to the very depression, anxiety, and fear that was borne out of the experiences I endured. I could have—but I didn't. Every ounce of life within us is capable of igniting the rocket of change and sending us soaring into a world we never imagined could exist. Every struggle, every ounce of pain, every wrong, and every loss is the undercurrent of strength you have been searching for. Stop shying away from those parts of your character you consider weaknesses and build them into your strengths. This isn't possible with waiting; it takes action. I wrote this book to help you gain perspective, to find your strength, to reimagine your life, to focus on your passion, and to identify the best version of yourself. I wrote this to help you take action.

My thoughts on perspective are supported by my personal experience, the shared experience of others, and the scientific research of many extraordinary people. This perspective has the potential to become foundational if you choose to learn it. I built my foundation in the aftermath of my greatest trial: the suicide of my father. While defiance led me to anger, sorrow, fear, and ignorance, I began to realize that I was blind to all the possibilities that lay beyond my emotions. This is not to suggest that my viewpoint toward emotion is negative; far from it, in fact. What I am asserting is that emotion has a way of constructing unseen obstacles that impede learning and development.

Your perspective is your reality. Your version of right may not be what other people see. Your version of right could be wrong to others. That is humanity. We live in a sophisticated paradox of subjective righteousness. However, regardless of who is right, the point still stands; you mostly only see one version of right. Yours. Yours is safe. It's comfortable. Your subconscious doesn't want to change anything because it is easier for the brain to function with the habits it already has. If depression, anxiety, and PTSD have been your normal for years then happiness is going to be taboo and uncomfortable for the brain. Perspective is the point of recognition when you do not have the habits to remain happy and healthy.

Perspective is the point of view from which you are looking at the object in focus. More often than not, our point of view is good enough. If you saw success from your perspective, then what reason would you have to change? The reality is that your brain, your family, even society, and many other things are trying to impose the idea that you're happy or successful where you are because it's the 'right' thing. What if you aren't happy or successful but you *are* doing the 'right' thing? Sometimes, placing the concept of right and wrong as the object in focus can change how we perceive our world for the better. Right and wrong are subjective and demand flexibility. If you remain rigid in your concept of right and wrong, your perspective will suffer and so will you. Life is about being rigid enough to respect the laws of nature and flexible enough to understand they are ever changing.

If your perspective is your reality, then your mindset is your learning curve. Mindset is determined by your mood every day. It is fluid. Perspective is built upon your flowing mindset; it is hardened by consistency. If you are locked in an environment that informs you that you're nothing more than a burden and worthless, where do you think your perspective will be constructed? Perspective is not built in a day. Your mindset is the daily foundation of how you perceive yourself and the world. The longer you are in negative environments, the worse you begin to feel. The environment around you then informs your reaction to it. Mindset is built in response to the environment we are exposed to and the experiences we face.

Mindsets like pessimism, optimism, and realism are perspectives that are learned. Most would agree that being around an extreme pessimist every day for a year would make life dark and dismal. The contrary, being around an extreme optimist for a year, might become quite annoying. Pessimism limits growth because one can rarely see value through the lens of negativity.

Optimism is problematic as it fundamentally asserts that things will 'work out' for the best in the long run. There is a lot of risk involved with hoping things work out for the best as life rarely complies with our hopes and ideals. There is a middle ground that can allow the best of both perspectives: Realism. Realism does not deny the existence of bad outcomes nor does it guarantee the eventuality of good ones. It simply focuses on accepting what has happened and concentrating on the importance of what comes next.

Realism is a solution focused perspective that harnesses the importance of choice. Every day, you are faced with choices. You can choose to create the habits that define your mindset. Either making the choice to limit yourself by thinking poorly of yourself or you can take a chance and believe in yourself—a choice that requires you to learn about what you are capable of. This learning is undertaken on a path riddled with pain, suffering, and doubt, but it is a path that starts and ends with choice. You may discover your perspective is getting in the way, but it is often only through expression that you are able to recognize this fact. Insert your pessimism, your optimism, even your realism here. Even realism can be a weakness when used improperly. Too much of a good thing can always be bad. Ultimately, perspective and mindset define the trajectory of our lives. If you want to change your trajectory, that is where you must begin.

Self-awareness is the key to unlocking change and growth. I was fortunately humble enough to realize, many times, that my perspective was preventing my growth. You cannot change or grow in a vacuum, however. There are two directions you can begin to reshape self-awareness: input and output. Inputting the knowledge of others looks like what you are doing right now. You can read, listen, or watch others. Read, listen, and watch enough of the 'right' stuff for you and change will happen depending on who you are consuming. You will know the people that speak to you. You know, the ones who say the same things others have said to you but they say it exactly the way you need to hear it. Social media has given us the ability to find those people easily but the obvious downside is that input is a one-way conversation. The reality is, you have a story to tell.

Output involves expressing yourself with the intention of gathering feedback. The goal is a discussion, not an argument. Express your story to the right people and you will see the lightbulbs in your mind start going off. Ideas will expand. Creative thought will ignite. Hope will ensue. For many, however, reliance on friends and family who are unprepared or uneducated is the reality. Self-awareness has a price. As you begin to express that story to others, you will begin to see people for who they are. You will see who supports you and who does not. Sharing your story will take courage to simply share but also to listen to the feedback that is returned. This is how a hardened perspective is reshaped: you put it out there for criticism and judgment. You will have people that betray your trust, demean your choices, and even deny your story. Bad things will happen because there are billions of people on the planet with their own sense of righteousness. Share a story with enough people and it will be subjected to people who do not agree.

I'm not suggesting you put your story in front of the worst critics you know. Instead, I am acknowledging that, as you begin to express yourself, you will find people who possess the empathy and understanding to help you renegotiate your story. It's about being tactical with who you choose to keep close. Expression is always benefited by the belief that every single moment in your life is important, and every single choice you make is inherently meaningful. When you tell people about your choices and omit critical details, they don't see the complete picture when they provide feedback. You must learn to believe, primarily, in your voice. You are the only person who has been and will be there for yourself 100% of your life. Every moment is important, but how you move forward changes your life. The choice to go out and tell your story to people is yours to make every single day.

Throughout the book, I will explain the stages of my own life and how my thinking has developed in response. I will reflect for you how my crises led me to build a growth-focused perspective. *Defy the Darkness* is a brutally honest account of my story and a deeply introspective examination of my emotions, experiences, and habits. In focus are the fundamentals of my thought process, which will illuminate the concepts of habit, mindset, and perspective. I will depict a cross-sectional view of the principles I held close, as well as the historical and cyclical nature of my choices. To complete my story, I will embed this examination in both the social realm and in the relevant research and stories of others. Every piece of supporting evidence helped me develop a deeper understanding of what I went through. The people involved and included in this book had an impact on me, whether I met them or not. There are still moments I am emotional about. Nevertheless, I believe emotions are the key to unlocking the soul. With that key, I wrote *Defy the Darkness* in an attempt to define the meaning behind my life and to help others grow in theirs.

My focus is on changing the world, one person at a time. I want you to learn how to survive when life beats you down. I want you to learn to focus on solving your problems instead of complaining about them. I want people to earn their own happiness by developing their best selves. People forget they have the choice to believe in themselves. I wrote this book because somewhere, someone needs help fighting the battles they won't tell anyone about. The goal of this book and of my life is simply this: I want to help others overcome their adversity. I want people to learn to express their story in a way that helps them live a life of meaning, and hopefully, to pay this gift forward to those beyond my direct reach. The choices involved in building happiness as a perspective are difficult to make. It isn't easy to choose yourself. It's painful to believe in yourself after you have spent so long feeling worthless. Yet you must begin. Join me and begin to choose yourself—choose to live a life worth living.

It is my hope that, together, we build a future generation of healthy-thinking individuals, high-performing people, and brilliant leaders. What follows is an account of my understanding of my life and of the pertinent research that exists today. I have been piecing together the work of others for many years in an attempt to understand myself. Let my quest for knowledge be your guiding light; learn from my mistakes. Throughout this book, my trials and defining moments in life show my own specific depiction of the world. Let this book be a shining example that persistence pays off. At the very least, you can follow that rule. Survive one more year, one more month, one more day, one more minute, or even one more second. No matter what it takes, tomorrow begins by surviving today.

Chapter 1

FUNDAMENTALS

The information that follows will require close reading, as there is significant value in each sentence. These fundamentals will offer perspective on everything that follows. You are about to gain a lot of important knowledge that can help you understand life and the human body and how the mind affects both. Please feel free to read and re-read if you must.

How we grow up may define our experiences, our strengths, and our weaknesses, but how we grow up does not need to affect where we end up. Everyone is faced with a choice: step forward and accept reality or hide from what hurts. Hiding from the truth causes issues; if not immediate, rest assured, the effects will show up down the road. I have, to date, not encountered a single exception to this rule. The reality is that life is long-term.

Unless our choices make it a reality, life rarely ends short. *Defy the Darkness*, much like life, is about choice. Choice does not require knowledge, though knowledge certainly helps, doesn't it? The question, then, is how do we choose wisely and live happily? We begin with the fundamentals.

The world is built upon fundamental knowledge. Whether in the form of a specific skill or general topic, there is always information that transcends. Anything from the mechanics of the human body to the mechanical workings of a machine, to the physics of gravity, inertia, and beyond exhibits these fundamental laws. Gravity, for example, is fundamental to my understanding of long-range shooting. The idea of what is fundamental is paramount to comprehension and development.

Fundamental knowledge is the hidden undercurrent that moves our world. Tapping into that knowledge is how we truly educate ourselves. Consider your greatest teachers and ask yourself if they were even professional teachers. How did the great teachers differentiate their teaching from others? Did they refer to a textbook to tell you the dates of historical events or list the rules of speech? Or did they, instead, delineate the fundamentals of how things are connected and explain the meaning behind how those things work? Human understanding blossoms when we define the *why*s and the *how*'s. Life can easily be compared to an iceberg—the vast majority unseen unless you know where to look. Everything you do comes with subtle nuances that affect how you choose and how you perform. Choosing to understand why we do what we do or how we can efficiently accomplish our goals has its own set of fundamentals. Those fundamental questions of *why* and *how* develop mindfulness and a perspective of growth.

I offer the importance of the fundamentals because they recur consistently in this book. Human development begins with the understanding of the various processes that take place internally and not those that occur externally. However, external events impact internal reactions and, therefore, must factor into any pursuit of understanding. I do not condone the notion that understanding the past provides all the answers to the future; I rather propose that defining the process of choice through reflection offers value. By reflecting on external events' impact, we can begin to filter out the major issues of humanity and deliver focused learning and development. We will look at the fundamental impact of my father's choice on my life in Chapter 2 and harness an understanding of how I built my mindset. The chapters of my life and the chapters of this book are an examination of the paths to development less traveled. However, these paths lead to unlocking your best self in every facet. To this end, I will begin with the fundamentals of understanding the lives of human beings from my personal perspective.

THE FORMULA

Life is built upon the accumulation of *time* and *experience* within an *environment*. In my understanding of life, these three are the most important fundamentals to understand your life: time, experience, and environment. While these three often represent the general facets of life attended to by social researchers, and for good reason as they essentially serve as the metrics of human life, this book is not statistical in nature. The three coincide completely and have immeasurable effects in every situation possible. This trinity defines human life and is an essential component of the reflection necessary to unlock the internal process. We look to these fundamentals to understand the biology of our choices. Due to our experiences in environments that differ, chemical and hormonal pathways are created over time. Consistency of emotions significantly affects those pathways.

Experiences are simply defined as the physical and cognitive events that happen to a human being. Your experiences may include being a specific race or gender, seeing death or trauma, having successes or failures, or managing the events that bring happiness or anger, among many others. The internal choices you make in defining yourself through those experiences are what we are attempting to understand. Why does one person's experience differ from another's? People often experience the same external events yet make drastically different internal choices. It is the development of these internal choices that leads to the long-term physical and cognitive habits and attitudes that begin to define personality. Experience is a broad topic; there are literally hundreds of thousands of studies vying to unlock greater understanding of the human experience. Experiences, however, don't happen in a vacuum. I realize this is an extraordinarily broad statement, but for practical purposes, it is our minds and bodies that begin to narrow down our experiences. (More on this later.)

Experiences are highly influenced by the environment in which they occur. Environment, in this context, is defined as the cognitive and physical space or setting in which a human being observes and interacts. Physical space is the general physical world that surrounds us and affects our neural intake, which refers to our senses of touch, taste, hearing, sight, and smell. We can take in approximately eleven million bits per second through our senses, but ten million are from sight alone. Cognitive environments are understood as mind spaces, defined by experiences across time. Simply put, they are thoughts and memories, and what we use to build our consciousness, mindset, and ultimately our perspective. Cognition is our choice processing of our neural intake. It is essentially how we *feel* about what our senses are taking in. Our subconscious mind manages approximately twenty million bits per second, but our conscious mind can only actively process approximately forty bits per second. That's right. You can only think at approximately forty bits per second, but you take in eleven million bits per second. This creates an interesting dilemma when it comes to how we fully experience our physical and cognitive environment, and how it leads to further questions. It bears repeating that many people experience the same external events, but in different environments and at different times in their lives, which is where the differentiation of choices begins.

The last paragraph was crucial for a couple reasons. There was a lot of dense information, so I'd like to break it down further: Even in the exact same scenario, no two people will have any real chance to feel the same forty bits every second through the same experience over time. There are eleven million things for them to choose from every second, and so many things that make a significant difference. Everyone has a history that defines for them what matters in every experience. You may love the color red, while someone else has a deep aversion to it. Your choices will reflect the forty bits you chose from the eleven million bits you had; someone else will select forty different things to consciously think about while you choose your own. This is an admittedly an over-simplified representation of how the mind works.

Researchers often observe people within their own environment through ethnographic studies and interviews in their own homes. Despite such intimacy, researchers sometimes fail to understand the cognitive spaces created by environments and past experiences. The real question is how, and for what reason, environment changes choice. The consistency of how the environment makes people feel is just a starting point. Another consideration is how human beings begin to reflect their environment in their personality to adapt to multiple environments. We mimic our environment to create easier transitions, but how and why do we transition through different mindsets based on our various environments and experiences? Mimicry makes living easier. Constantly standing out from what is normal is emotionally taxing; the energy expended by disrupting everyday experiences begins to fatigue the mind and body. But that is just one reason, and there are literally thousands of answers to that single question. Experiences and environments are far more complex than they are credited with being. Time only enhances this complexity.

Time, in this context, refers to the sequential order of experiences in specific environments, maturity at age, and the biological timeline of life. The time in which we are alive is more specifically categorized by the periods of transition through maturity hence the categorization of infancy, adolescents, childhood, preteens, teens, young adults, adults, elderly. Choice is defined differently as we mature, and we know we should no longer make the choices we did as a child. Our consciousness achieves different heights based on our experiences and doesn't necessarily come down to our age. Each person operates at a unique level of consciousness, which is derived from their genetics and the experiences that impacted their life. At every turn, the current mental programming defines the next moment, and choices and internal reactions within the context of experiences and environment offer many moments to instantly separate ourselves from what other people think and feel. This is why life becomes so complex. The sequential order of experiences that happen within a specific environment leads to massive differentiation of choice. No two lives are ever the same.

To add to the complex nature of time, generations are different when it comes to culture and technology. An adult living in 1990 could be fundamentally different than one living in 2020. This complicates research in part because the baseline of normal is constantly adapting to the ever-increasing technological and cultural transformation. What also changes over time is the perception of thought within environments, such as a society. Such large-scale transitions of social development happen over time in environments and deliver never-before-seen experiences. The idea of texting while driving didn't exist in the 1990s, for example. What we can determine is that time is the constant. The environment in which we live and the experiences we are reduced to are situated along this linear track of time. Time is linear, while experiences and environment are three-dimensional in form.

Given enough time, a person can accumulate a vast number of experiences and observe and interact in myriad environments. Certain experiences and environments are subject to the fundamental idea we are attempting to understand: the idea of choice. People may not choose to experience certain things, and we must bear in mind that some choices are strengthened socially. The idea of choice complicates our understanding of human trajectory. Some humans are subject to experiences and environments without having a choice, while others are given the choice. Babies don't get to decide who their parents will be, whereas parents can make a choice to keep or abandon a baby. Tragedy often comes without choice for those who suffer it. Of interest about experience is that it can have a compounding effect in a way that you learn from those experiences, and a non-compounding effect in the way that you forget over time. Time, again, is the constant. Time is unchanging and unwavering; we are bound to it and pulled along by it, whether we like it or not.

By now, you have likely come to appreciate that the fundamentals are complex. The reality is that we create fundamentals as a framework for the incredibly complex structures within which we interact. Fundamentals are a way to simplify life. My background in shooting and firearms instruction is a perfect example. Shooting is often broken down into four fundamentals. As you advance into more precise levels of accuracy, many of the best shooters will begin to add varying fundamentals to expose more of the complexity. It's hard to teach someone to shoot two miles away by saying, "Just get into a steady position, start a breathing cycle, ensure proper sight picture, and perform good trigger control." I'm sure there are many shooters out there who wish it was that simple! The fact is that those fundamentals make no sense unless they are better explained and with more complexity. For now, let's move from the fundamentals of understanding life to understanding ourselves and our bodies.

The general rule is: People require specific experiences to survive, adapt and grow, and to control their mindset. New experiences are scientifically proven to be vital for learning and growth. The pain and confusion felt in the brain from learning a new skill is your brain adapting. It does this by firing electrical synapses down a new neural pathway. That's called growth. Growth mindsets aren't premonitions, smoke and mirrors, or even magic. Growth mindsets take work, as you are reimagining and adapting your brain as it attempts to do something it doesn't yet know how to do. Growth mindsets are built; they are not genetically made. That's science. They are not bestowed upon a baby at birth; they are forged in the environments in which we live and by the experiences that force us to adapt. Choice can be a detriment: too much, or not enough, choice can have negative effects. If humans don't receive experiences that force them to adapt, there is no contextual reason for them to adapt. In some circumstances, we need to be taught. This is what becomes fundamental about this book: we derive emotions from our experiences and environments. Emotions link environments, experiences, and time. If the emotions that motivate, challenge, inspire, or force us to adapt are not inputted into our systems, changing in general becomes difficult.

Alan Watkins, in _Coherence_, builds this dimension of physiology into the idea of choice. Choice, as Watkins asserts, has any number of different effects on the human body.[1] Positive choices of gratitude and appreciation create a concoction of enhancing hormones. Negative ideation delivers cortisol, which directly inhibits the body in several ways. For one, cortisol is one of the main reasons people with depression have such a difficult time moving past it; stress creates cortisol and cortisol enhances depression, while depression creates additional cortisol. This is a vicious cycle that is broken only by making difficult choices and often only after months, if not years, of struggle. Cortisol has also been linked to the development of bad cholesterol in multiple studies. Stress ignites the part of the brain that manages the body's fight-or-flight responses: the amygdala. The amygdala then boosts the production of hormones that often go unused, since we no longer run from lions. There is a reason why heart disease has become the leading cause of death in America. Stress has everything to do with it. The human body no longer functions in the environment in which we evolved. We are physiologically unaccustomed to modern-day life and our experiences are now being computed, as Watkins would say, on outdated software.

Bessel Van der Kolk, a prestigious psychiatrist, wrote the book, _The Body Keeps the Score,_ which has contributed a practical understanding of how therapy has developed both in the scientific and social realm.[2] Van der Kolk defines a holistic approach to understanding

---

[1]   Watkins, Alan, *Coherence: The Secret Science of Brilliant Leadership.*

[2]   Van der Kolk, Bessel, *The Body Keeps the Score: Brain, Mind, and Body in the Healing of Trauma.*

how to help people while defining the integral pieces of the body most aptly effected. Every case is different; however, trauma is a highly common occurrence in many people's lives. Trauma is important because it physically, not just emotionally, changes the brain.

Alongside the work of Dr. Van der Kolk, Peter Levine addresses the idea of bodily conditioning attached to trauma.[3] Trauma initiates the fight, flight, freeze, and feign responses within the amygdala which is part of the limbic system. The limbic system itself is most commonly understood to manage things like emotions and memory. With that being said, we process the eleven million bits of information from our five senses every second through the amygdala. Based on past experience, the amygdala makes choices on what is and is not a threat *before* the neo-cortex has the opportunity to impart its logic. If you have faced trauma in your past, your amygdala will begin to misinterpret threats. For example, it is commonly understood that veterans of war react to things like fireworks as if they were still at war. From my two deployments to Afghanistan, that reaction isn't a choice, it's a body response that can't be controlled until it is physically and emotionally addressed. War, of course, is a small portion of the trauma that exists in today's world. Things like sexual trauma, rape, abuse, bullying, accidents, murder, sex trafficking, and so much more exist every day that are rarely supported nearly as

---

[3] Levine, Peter, *Waking the Tiger: Healing Trauma*.

much as veterans. Both Levine and Van der Kolk offer clearly defined paths forward.

Levine's work centers on trauma recovery with a particular focus on renegotiating the actual emotion stored in the body from the past trauma. Although he diverges from the majority of health professionals, in _Waking the Tiger_, Levine asserts that trauma arouses instincts from the reptilian part of the brain, emotions from the mammalian part, and rational/logical thought from the neocortex. Each part of the brain reacts to the energy of trauma by interpreting it in its own way. If the reptilian part of the brain is not allowed to discharge the survival energy, Levine posits that the other two integral parts of the brain are altered and become out of sync. Reenacting the past trauma and renegotiating how the body managed the trauma the first time offers a way to bring the system back in sync.

Levine's book acts as a catalyst for the idea that re-negotiating the internal processes with choice creates a better life for those who suffer from trauma. Although, the process can be understood without trauma and therefore can be used to re-negotiate just about anything. Your story becomes the focus and to reshape your habits and mindset, the idea is to begin re-writing your story. Changing how you perceive the details is paramount. While attempting to understand the context and definitions you have brought forward allows you to decipher who you have become and therefore makes the changes necessary.

William Glasser introduces a psychological dimension in his aptly titled *Choice Theory*.[4] Glasser explains the premises of choice theory by stating:

> "Choice Theory® is based on the simple premise that every individual only has the power to control themselves and has limited power to control others. Applying Choice Theory allows one to take responsibility for one's own life and at the same time, withdraw from attempting to direct other people's decisions and lives. Individuals are empowered to take responsibility for their choices and support others in taking ownership of their choices. Negative behaviors reduce in frequency and intensity, relationships strengthen and satisfaction in life increases."[5]

The world is dominated by what is referred to as external control theory, which implies that we have some form of control or ownership of others. Choice theory is defined as the opposite: People do not have any control or ownership of others and thus must learn to understand and focus on internal control of their own thought processes and choices. The basis of human misery

---

[4]   Glasser, William, *Choice Theory: A New Psychology of Personal Freedom*.

[5]   "What Is Choice Theory?" *Glasser Institute for Choice Theory*, August 20, 2019, https://wglasser.com/what-is-choice-theory/ 4 January 2021.

and suffering is mostly focused on bad relationships, according to Glasser. We've all been there, haven't we? Husband or wife, mom or dad, brother or sister, maybe friend or classmate, we all have those people throughout life that impact us negatively. Some are more subtle than others. The point is our relationships matter more than we care to believe.

Watkins, Levine, Van der Kolk, and Glasser each offer a fundamental sense of understanding regarding the process of living a happy life. Gary Vaynerchuk, Simon Sinek, Tony Robbins, and many other renowned entrepreneurs and motivators are living examples of how the fundamentals of these works can be harnessed. Choice is the underlying fundamental and serves as the focus of this book. I began writing *Defy the Darkness* after years of trying to understand other people's choices. What I ultimately learned is simple: The only choice that matters is your own. When we analyze another person's choices, we seek to understand things well beyond our comprehension. In doing so, we attempt to analyze an entire lifetime's worth of experiences within environments that weren't likely to include ourselves. Furthermore, as each experience and environment imprints upon a person, the body adds its own conditioning, which is then categorized as a recurring reaction. Mental choice doesn't always align with physical reaction, which introduces additional complexity. Basically, you shouldn't judge others for their choices because it is impossible for you to understand the reasons that initiated those choices.

Likewise, you should never allow the judgment of others to control your own choices. It is physically impossible for them to gain access to the context that is locked within your mind.

I learned that the hard way as you will learn. I blamed others for where I ended up and quite frankly, I wasn't wrong. The reality is I wasn't right either. I blamed and I judged without really thinking it through. Part of life is what happens to you, can't really escape that part. Another part is how you react to what happens to you. That's choice. My dad was going to die eventually. I could absolutely blame him for the time he took from me. I could also judge those around me for not doing more to help me. I could blame society for not having better resources available for a kid like me. Where would all that blame and judgment lead me? By highlighting those judgments and that blame, I would be minimizing the best parts of myself that I could be sharing with the world. I would be making the same choice my father made in a different context. I'd be alive and people would know the best I have to offer but they would only see the depressed, spiteful, and angry version of me. Instead of looking out, I learned to look deep within. To do so, I had to learn how to understand my life and frame my narrative.

Each of the authors I mentioned earlier as well as my background in sociology has brought me to understand that there is an equation to understand human life. Life equals experiences in environments over time. My equation for understanding life would be quite simple if life was only physical. Of course, it is not that simple. There is an unknown variable that only you can map and that is what is in your mind. Your cognitive spaces and experiences are the missing variables. What this means is my equation is mathematically useless because no one will ever know how to solve for your x and y (cognitive experiences and environments). This equation isn't for mathematicians, it's for you. Only you can begin to use it to understand your life. This tool may not speak to you, but it will speak to someone and that's why it's here. Your choices inside and out are the context you need to put together. Maybe this formula can begin to help with that.

$$Life = \frac{[(Experiences\ Physical\ and\ Cognitive) + (Environments\ Physical\ and\ Cognitive)]}{Time}$$

There is, of course, more to *Defy the Darkness* than understanding choice. You will join me on my journey through life and observe my choices as I endeavor to explain what compelled me to create my own happiness from the struggles I endured. I have written this book to share my hard-fought knowledge with those in need. If you know someone who has struggled with suicide, trauma, death, abuse, depression, anxiety, PTSD . . . I beg you to share this book with them. My unending goal in life is to save people from themselves by offering them a glimpse of the greatness that lies within them. I want people to realize the potential they don't yet recognize and expand their perspective on life itself. But what is most important to me is the final choice in this book: the choice to live. There is no sweeter gift than life; everyone is worthy of receiving that gift. My only request is that you defy the darkness within yourself and choose to live.

This framework focuses on understanding how the aforementioned fundamentals apply to my life. More specifically, I will focus on my choices, which I have created, and that have impacted my life. I am a practitioner. I have done what I am advising you to do. Each choice was created in its own time and place for the purpose of creating the best me I can be. I am no better than you, and I will never be. What I am is constantly progressing. Every person on this planet has the potential to be their own great, but achieving this unique greatness comes down to choices. I firmly believe in the potential residing within every single one of us. This empathetic belief fosters a deeper understanding of the fundamentals of life. I attempt to see an individual's framework before I expose them to the truth of their life. I offer honesty and clarity. Your life should not be wasted hiding from the worst things you've lived through. Your worst experiences are where your strength lies.

I offer to you my opinions on how to transform your greatest weaknesses and most difficult moments into the manifestation of strength. One of my many goals is to show you how you can choose to be the strongest version of yourself. I want you to renegotiate your pain, your stress, and your struggle to create a launchpad for your dreams. I want you to help yourself, and others, become stronger and smarter every single day. The most important fundamental I can offer you is choice. Choose what you want. Choose how you want to achieve it. Choose to be different. Choose to accept or not. Live your life by your own choices and stop allowing your past to choose your future. Choose to live in a way that makes you happy. Most importantly, choose to live.

This will not be easy. The struggle is ongoing, and you cannot achieve greatness without sacrifice. You must invest your time and your energy. In fact, you will have to expend a vast amount of both to become what you want to be. Prepare yourself for a grind that will never cease. Learn to embrace challenging emotions. Fall in love with being uncomfortable. You will have to face your darkness, your depression, or your anxiety. Inspiration doesn't come from music, movies, books, or speeches. Determination doesn't come from your coach, your mom, your dad, or your friends. Motivation doesn't come from heroes and heroines, role models, or even this book . . .

It comes from you making the choice to act.

Chapter 2

FIND A SOLUTION

A solution-focused mindset cannot be defeated. Those people who continuously find ways to move forward, to progress, and to fight their way through any situation succeed in whatever they put their mind to. This rule has become a mantra: "Understand the problem, find a solution." The only requirement is an unwillingness to ever quit.

The unfolding of my life seemed to happen in an instant that was burned into my memory. Few moments in life hit you harder than the ones you have no control over. The experience of being absolutely helpless seems to instill something in people that cannot be found anywhere else. Every single day, people experience moments of helplessness and events that will continue to haunt them throughout their lives. Depending on the timing, these are the moments charged with extraordinary potential or heartbreaking burden. In seconds, the whole world can flow into a single uncontrollable moment that changes your life.

People continually, and inadvertently, make decisions that have drastic effects on their lives. The choices of a drunk driver at the wheel, a child who follows a ball into the street, or a man on the brink who believes he is a burden all have profound effects upon the world. Yet, people often fail to appreciate the gravity of their choices. Our world is an ever-growing result of the choices of everyone around us. Your environment can shift from a state of contentment to chaos and leave you feeling unsafe, speechless, terrified, depressed, anxious, and so on. *Overcoming* becomes the marker of success and failure yet is rarely understood or discussed. Defining and redefining struggle is, therefore, internalized in the depths of our minds. We are left to "figure it out" or "deal with it," regardless of our age or temperament. For all intents and purposes, we are cast out to sea during a hurricane and are expected to somehow survive without the benefit of a life vest.

We all endure hardships and face difficult times. Those who have never felt the pain don't understand how difficult a single moment can be. People who have felt the pain cannot forget the moment, even if they try to act as if it never happened by living a lie and distancing themselves from the embarrassment, shame, disgrace, fear, or the hatred involved. We try to seem normal, but in those moments, we ignite a process similar to that of the phoenix. We initiate a perpetual rising from the ashes after our multiple mighty falls into despair. Too often, people continue in this cycle without an understanding of how to overcome it. Redefining mindset is the beginning of the process that will change our perspective—and a change in perspective establishes a new self-image.

If overcoming is the goal, then the difference between success and failure rests primarily on how you choose to react and, secondarily, how you tell the story. True success is determined by a thought process, the greatest motivators and leaders on the planet assert. Positive or negative, the way you tell your story determines much about who you are. Thoughts dominate our self-image, and habitual thinking often reveals how you see yourself. Self-image plays a major role in how you learn, adapt, and overcome, and it determines your perspective. Perspective, put simply, is what you believe is probable, possible, and impossible. The pairing of your self-image with your perspective often determines your mindset. Mindset is fluid and ever changing; it forms your learning curve as your emotions affect you daily. To begin the process of changing how you think, you must first determine how you view yourself, define your perspective, and understand the true nature of your mindset. To change, we must begin with how we understand problems and solutions.

There are two prevailing schools of thought. The majority of people are problem focused. My hypothesis is that social consumption of modern news media and its commitment to a misguided, "If it bleeds, it leads . . ." strategy is responsible for this prevalence. Trauma, after all, is humanity's drug of choice. It's easy to distinguish people who ascribe to the other school of thought; the people who focus on solving problems and who are often highly efficient performers. This is not to say that solution-focused thinkers don't find themselves focusing on the problems of life; they simply don't often get hung up on them for long. There is a process to understanding how to think through problems and find solutions. Focusing on the problem is the first step but to move beyond, you then need to stop focusing on the problem. Human beings can only think so much. Overthinking, in my experience, comes from trauma.

It comes from being placed in extraordinary circumstances and not given the support to reconcile them. Trauma creates a constant state of arousal. In my experience, that mental arousal seems to be attempting to make up for not being able to prevent the circumstances of the past. My father's death taught me that but it has certainly been confirmed with the hundreds and thousands I have interacted with. Problems aren't the problem. It's how you were trained to think about problems that are. The next section will develop a new way of defining problems but to truly transform, self-awareness is the key. Open the door to what informs your decisions. Why do you think the way that you think? What moments in your life taught you to think that way?

Keep these questions in the back of your mind as you read through my version of problem solving. They will be addressed later on.

PROBLEM SOLVING 101

To find a solution, rely on a three-step process: *evaluate, isolate, act*. Each step of this process is defined by how our mind processes information. It is simple yet not something that can be easily mastered. As with much of the work that I do, simplicity works only if you have the willingness to do the work. In other words, it is hard, but it is possible. Evaluating problems is something that humans are incredibly adept at, hence why we have built our societies, cities, governments, etc. It is how we evaluate the "emotional" and "human" problems that have become the bane of our existence. I will help you understand some of the relevant context behind that but also give you a more defined second step: isolation. Isolating things we can change and what we cannot is almost more important than evaluation. When we have clearly isolated what we can do and what we can't, action becomes much more clearly defined and clinical.

To evaluate, you must consider the problem within the context of the process and within the realm of your own physiology. If you are having trouble with your car, you must evaluate the vehicle within the context of mechanical engineering. Context matters. Process matters. Evaluating the problem within a relationship cannot be done without first understanding how both people came together while simultaneously understanding how they fundamentally define the process of a relationship. Human beings are "meaning making" creatures, which means we rely dramatically on how we define the things around us. People will hold onto things that harm them by creating a definition of why they need it. We are built to develop meaning. When evaluating problems, focus on the meaning. Meaning is understood through the lens of our definitions and our context.

Problems are not simply understood by logic, however. Problems compound stress, which is why evaluation is not the only step in the process. As we begin to evaluate the problem, the mind tends to jump ahead of what is considered logical. Thinking about the meeting you could miss in two weeks because your car might be in the shop is certainly practical, but it's not likely to be the case. If you compound your problem with things that could happen, you will overload your brain. Let me repeat that for those in the back, you *will* overload your brain. Anxiety comes from unsustainable amounts of fear, worry, and uncertainty that ultimately force your body to react by elevating your heart rate, increasing your breathing, among other things to support your brain working overtime to think of how to save you from the uncertainty. If your anxiety is linked to past trauma, your fear could kick in a full-blown flashback.

Evaluation must cease when it steps outside the bounds of the context and the process, hence the need for isolation. As we evaluate, it is necessary to isolate the problem to its first-line effects while also maintaining control of our physiology. To do so, focus your thoughts on what you are realistically able to do. Anxiety is most often induced by our own thoughts rather than outside issues. To manage yourself, you must practice thinking. Remember that controlling your heart rate allows you to logically focus. Deep breathing is the best way to manage your emotional state which thus becomes the best way to retain your logic. Begin asking yourself the questions listed below. If the answers lead you to believe you are worrying too deeply, stressing, or are in a state of fear, then you must focus on one thing before stepping into logic: Breathing.

Isolation-focused Questions

1.) What can I do right now to stop this problem from getting worse?
2.) Why is this problem happening?
3.) Am I part of the problem? If so, what is that I am doing that makes me part of the problem?
4.) Are my emotions allowing me to think logically about what is happening?
5.) Am I breathing normally or am I elevating? If elevating, how can I ground myself?
6.) Am I looking too far ahead and not actually dealing with the problem?

7.) What am I actually doing?

8.) Is this problem something I cannot control?

The last question is probably one of the most important questions you can ask yourself. In life, we will face millions of problems. Many of them are solvable, but there are probably more that are far outside our control. We can't always solve every problem. There is a reason the phrase, "Hindsight is 20/20" exists in the English language. If we knew what we knew today, we could have solved the problems of yesterday. It isn't realistic to think we can solve yesterday's problems. Yesterday has become context. Today is about action. That action is about preventing the same problems from happening again.

Choosing to act is the final step in the process, though isolation is arguably the most important. Evaluation allows us to practice looking at problems objectively, but isolating our thoughts is how we actually achieve objectivity. Too often, people react before understanding the problem; they focus on emotions. Being able to isolate your thoughts and feelings allows you to act with a clear mind. It is easy to relinquish control of our thoughts and emotions, sending that angry email or passive-aggressive text. It is more difficult to maintain patience to fully understand the context of what is happening. I can tell you from experience that patience almost always leaves you feeling better in the long run. Regret comes from acting without control or without the complete picture.

Action can mean so many different things in the context of problem-solving. In some cases, it means pulling up your sleeves and getting the working down. When the flood waters begin to rise, you start filling sandbags and protecting what you can. At times, there will be problems so large, you have no ability to stop the inevitable. Fill all the sandbags you want but Hurricane Katrina wasn't going to be stopped. When you realistically look at the problem something like that presents, damage control becomes the action. And when that paramedic finds that person in the wreckage who has lost too much blood, no amount of CPR will bring them back . . . accepting the inevitability of death is the action. If there is a law of life that manifests itself more than all the others, it is this: You will lose. Whether it is a game, a job, a house, a friend, or a father, you will lose. The next action is to evaluate that problem, isolate what you can change, and move live for the ones we have lost. Sometimes our actions look like doing nothing, but the reality is the action is to adapt the way we think.

One of these steps does not create a problem-solving mindset, all these together create that mindset. A mindset requires habits to be formed and perspectives to change. If you are in a place you don't want to be in while you are reading this book, is part of the problem your perspective? I don't know. That isn't my question to answer. What I do know is that if you blame others for your misfortune, then you are creating a problem within your perspective that infects everything in your life. Negativity of that magnitude permeates into every crack and crevice of your being and people will walk away. They will tell you all sorts of reasons, but it all leads to one thing: you are too distracted with blaming others for your failures to address the things you must change about yourself.

I don't say this to hurt you or put you down. I say this from experience. I did this myself. For nineteen years I was distracted by my father's choice, always blaming him for my misfortune. I lied to myself, telling myself I was where I was because of him. I was suffering, no doubt. The reality is simple though. I created my perception of him whether it was conscious or not. I was part of the problem. I created the silence. I created the self-destructive thoughts you will hear in this book. I constructed my downfall just as much as I orchestrated my rise. You are going to face hard truths in your life, learn this one now: You are a part of every problem. Are you going to add to the problem or become part of the solution? Choose the easy wrong, or the hard right.

Solving simple problems isn't difficult. Solving life's problems is different. We sometimes find ourselves moving through life stressed and overburdened, and without the opportunity to begin evaluating our problems. The key is matching mindset, perspective, and self-image to what we want them to be. As you will note in the following example, the trinity of evaluate, isolate, and act is paramount to becoming your version of success.

As you follow, try to imagine what it was like for me to evaluate, isolate, and act upon the problems I faced.

DEATH COMES FOR US ALL

It was early on a beautiful August morning when I came down the stairs. My father stepped into the kitchen saying something about a meeting that would run late that night, and that we likely wouldn't see him until the next day. To be honest, my recollection is vague about what exactly he said at that point. I was, after all, only six years old. What isn't vague, however, is the undeniable feeling that came over me as I listened to him and watched his demeanor. I remember the feeling in the pit of my stomach as my father spoke. His eyes told me everything I needed to know. I would never see him again. What I didn't know was how to put that feeling into words. Even now, I honestly don't know how to describe the feeling.

I will never forget my father's final lie: "I love you. I'll see you tomorrow." His eyes told me the truth, and a torrent of emotion flowed through me. My intuition was sending up every red flag possible. My heart was pounding, and multiple powerful emotions overcame me simultaneously. It may sound unbelievable, but I truly knew I would never see him again. My instinct drove me to reach out to him, to stop him from leaving, and to never let go of him. I grabbed his leg, sobbing. Through intermittent wails, I remember telling him not to leave. Over and over again, I begged him. Every ounce of me was screaming for him to stay. It was one of the only times in my life that I felt truly powerless.

I can still feel his six-foot-seven-inch frame pulling me off with ease and leaving me to watch him walk out the door. To this day, I don't know how he kept his composure, knowing what he was about to do. He was supposed to meet with a psychiatrist that day, and he likely would have been diagnosed with bipolar disorder and depression; yet he chose a different path. He chose the path less traveled by driving to a secluded park and firing a shot with his hunting rifle. By ending his life, he instantly altered my path and the paths of everyone who knew him. It was a moment that would tear me apart, and in a context, more difficult to manage than if he had simply died in an accident. I was left with an enormous burden that I forced myself to bear: the burden of guilt. That moment left me scarred because I viewed my father's choice as rejection. My mind made it a more traumatic event by taking upon myself the responsibility—and self-blame—that I didn't try hard enough to stop him. My immaturely developed logic couldn't control the brunt of the emotional chaos that developed in the wake of my father's suicide. That simple choice shattered my perspective, my mental health, and my life. I was broken.

My father's suicide triggered a series of events that led me to where I find myself today. I wholeheartedly believe there is no possible way I would have become the man I am without his choice. That choice affected me so profoundly, I have no concept of how my life could have been different. I can't even picture what might have happened. There were many moments in which I struggled with believing there *could be* a life without him. A boy without a father, I believed, would always be a boy. Who would teach me to live dangerously and love recklessly? Who would play catch with me? Who would model for me the intricacies of being a good man? A good father? Who would teach me how to grow up? I had a million questions and no answers. For years, I felt I had nothing but weaknesses, because my friends weren't as emotional; my friends hadn't been broken. Many of them had both parents and no experience with such deeply scarring trauma. No one I knew had nightmares so vivid, they refused to go back to sleep for fear of reliving the trauma. The kids around me just weren't exposed to the same pain.

I don't have many strong memories of the years that immediately followed my father's death. I survived. Even at my tender age, that was what I learned to do. Survival has a way of channeling your mental energy into exhaustive analytical and emotional thinking. *How do I survive today?* became a question I asked daily. I had little idea of how to ask for help, and no idea of how to respond. Adults would tell that it wasn't reasonable to hold onto guilt but wouldn't often provide reasons why. Often, my mother or sister would listen to me cry in the bathroom from outside the locked door while my brain shuffled through an entire life's worth of decisions I was going to have to make without my father. Instead of sleeping a full eight hours, I would think for five to six hours and sleep for three. I would analyze what happened repeatedly. This, of course, led me to get used to only sleeping two to three hours each night. I could rarely make sense of my father's choice, which would repeatedly lead me to sorrowful breakdowns, fits of rage, and genuine depression. Most of these breakdowns happened out of sight and out of mind of my family, by my choice.

I found myself diving deeper into believing that I was bound to repeat my father's mistakes. I came from him; therefore, I was bound to become him. I established a self-fulfilling prophecy, it turns out. In my mind, I had no other options, but there were a lot of questions: namely, *how long will it take for me to break my promises to myself?* It seemed the one redeeming quality I had inherited from my parents was my stubbornness. Having endured so much already, pain was a very different animal for me than it was for others. My stubbornness only made it easier to wrestle with, and my analytical mindset in fact assisted me in developing additional ways to be more stubborn. The longer I survived, the more I began to entertain the hope of overcoming my father's choice. It was these miniscule recreations that began to prop up my principles with optimism. Day by day, survival became the general key to my living.

I was thrust into, arguably, one of the most torturous moments any six-year-old could face. I was given an advantage in life experience and depth of thought, but I didn't look at it that way. Instead, I assumed—

and continued to, for most of my life—that I was at a disadvantage. I played into that. I was a victim of suicide, but I also rarely told anyone. I lost my father, and no one could bring him back. It broke me to know that I had lost someone so instrumental in my life. It wouldn't dawn on me to think about how much I had in fact learned from this event until much later. The feelings that cluttered my mind had left no space for analytical logic. I looked at the glass half-empty or half-full when I really should have understood that I wasn't holding a glass; I was holding a fifty-five-gallon drum above my head and thinking I could manage it all my life. I was simply too young and unprepared. Looking back, I was in fact rebuilding myself. It was a slow process, but I was reforming my thoughts every day. I was redefining my story every chance I got. I had to begin to rethink my perspective on my problems, and it turns out my problem wasn't the fact that my father had committed suicide but rather that I believed I was a guilty party while also feeling like a victim.

Immediately following my father's suicide, I began to formulate small character traits that allowed me to maintain my survival. I fostered a mindset of adopting small claims of optimism to lift me up, while also playing the stubbornness card when I had no optimism available to grasp. I fell back on one of the most important concepts of my life: I learned to find comfort in the uncomfortable. Pain, I realized, never really goes away. Pain is the hell within you. You either learn to control it, or it controls you. The very first thing I began to overcome was thinking logically during uncomfortable or painful situations. It would start with the emotional pain linked to my situation. I had to learn to control my emotions through breathing before I could think clearly. Unfortunately, most of my breakdowns became internal wars of attrition because I was fighting between my neocortex and my amygdala's learned response of guilt and shame. No one wins in a war of attrition. I eventually burned myself out from thinking. I rarely spoke, but I was always an intense thinker. The first years were the hardest, filled with many powerful feelings and almost no control.

Finding comfort in what is uncomfortable changes the kind of thought that is summoned. People in uncomfortable situations tend to misread their emotions for legitimate logical thought. Emotion is the energy your body receives from the surrounding environment and circumstances. When your mind begins to formulate a response to that energy, feelings are generated. These definitions originate from Dr. Alan Watkins, author of *Coherence: The Secret Science of Brilliant Leadership*. Dr. Watkins studies human performance in a decidedly physiological way. The importance of defining the difference between emotion and feeling comes into play when we begin to understand what Dr. Watkins refers to as conditioning: "Conditioning is an automatic survival and learning mechanism...the purpose of this automatic response is to evaluate threats to our survival and trigger a response that keeps us alive." (95) For my own application, conditioning becomes important when we look at how we respond to life situations. It is the beginning of the redefining process and how we begin to retell our story. My father's suicide conditioned my feelings of guilt and shame, which became responsible for my reaction to any conversation I would have about it.

Reactive thinking often leads to mistakes as a result of this kind of thought not being filtered through our neocortex. Call to mind a moment in your recent past when you became very angry, upset, or sad. Did you choose the logical route? Or the emotional one? Did you feel like there was a better response after the fact? I view emotion as a stream. When you aren't actively feeling any defining emotion, the stream bed is mostly dry and controlled with a more passive emotion. When angered, upset, saddened, etc., your body is attempting to formulate an overdose of responses and the stream quickly overflows. We all have limits that are in a constant state of transition. The human mind has the potential to handle extraordinary amounts of pain and suffering, but not without training. How well the mind handles pain and suffering is dependent on how you train your conscious and subconscious thought to react to feelings brought about by your emotional environment. In short, life is all about controlling your feelings.

This is the moment in the book when I tell you how important it is to fall back on the biological fundamentals of the human brain. Emotions, as we already know, is energy in motion (Thanks again to Dr. Watkins). Emotion is energy—a biological energy determined by what our body is experiencing. We largely cannot control the emotion we experience, save by changing our environment. However, feelings are entirely different. I am repeating this knowledge, as it is absolutely vital to recognize that, for a majority of human beings, feelings are a choice. We have the ability to control what we feel and how we feel, but this does require learning how the brain is conditioned.

Why do I discuss emotions and feelings in a chapter about solving problems? The answer is simple: Think about how much time we waste being angry or upset about the things that happen to us, instead of immediately moving to fix the problem. We spend countless hours a month being upset about things that are often completely out of our control. Additionally, those very things can often be solved relatively quickly without any frustration. The question becomes: Is there a benefit to being upset? To some, anger or frustration is a conditioned response to the problems of life. That anger and frustration, however, induces the creation of cortisol (the stress hormone). Remember that cortisol is thought to be the precursor to heart disease, which is currently the leading cause of death in America. Emotion clouds judgment and reduces our ability to make logical decisions. Dr. Watkins even describes that anger can literally cut off the connection between the amygdala and the neocortex, which actually prevents an immediate logical decision.

Our emotions are undeniable, but our feelings are controllable. Control requires practice, and practice requires knowledge. Books like *Defy the Darkness* are just the beginning. The key to controlling your feelings is managing your breathing, according to Dr. Watkins. Why, though? Breathing manages the most electromagnetically charged organ in the human body, the organ that synchronizes every other organ—the heart. Control of our feelings is predicated on our ability to control our physiology. The heart is the distribution center for hormones, including cortisol. Therefore, if you lose control of your heart, you lose control of stress. Rhythmic breathing is the solution to almost any problem.

LONG SHOT

Now, I am a problem-solver. I don't walk into a situation with the mindset of expressing the first emotions that hit me. I walk into every situation as a calm and collected, focused individual. Throughout twenty years of suffering, learning to focus on breathing redefined my problem-solving abilities. Mental breakdowns that would last for hours when I was a child and teen became shorter in duration as soon as I learned of the benefits of breathing. I first learned of breathing around aged nineteen, when I began to teach myself how to shoot long-range. In stressful situations, shooters must limit the effect of their heartbeat on the rifle. To minimize error, smooth, rhythmic breathing creates a more stable platform to take important shots. The longer the distance, the more every single element affects the shot—from the gun, to the shooter, to the environment, to the bullet itself. A movement as minor as a heartbeat can be the difference between hitting or missing.

I began shooting long-range after I returned from basic training. Back then, 300 yards was as far as I knew how to shoot; that was what the Army taught me. Today, I shoot targets beyond 1,000 yards and often teach people to shoot 1,000 yards in a matter of a couple of hours. The vast number of variables that affect long-range shooting requires intense and calculated analytical thinking; it requires you to mentally check off possible weaknesses within your fundamentals, the rifle's structure, the ammunition, the ballistic solution, and finally the environmental data. A single element can ruin a shooting session, which can throw large amounts of time and money down the drain. It's frustrating. It requires failure, and that is truly humbling. Long-range shooting honed my ability to analyze and isolate the problem step-by-step, and then solve the problem. Thinking outside the box of long-range shooting and applying the fundamentals to other forms of shooting such as handguns and carbines allowed me to reimagine how I applied myself to the firearm and how that connection brought about accuracy. I formulated mental checklists built from analyzing things that often went wrong and then applied myself to solving those problems.

First, I always began with myself. I learned to dry fire so much that my body knew when it made a mistake. The old anecdote that says, "Amateurs work to get it right, professionals work until they can't get it wrong" definitely applied to me. I worked until it was rare for me to get it wrong; but when something did go wrong, I always first blamed myself. Blaming myself humbled me; it controlled my emotional output, because I knew it was something I could fix. I took ownership of me. Blaming myself allowed me to be positive about overcoming the problem because it became a challenge. If I were to blame everything else before me, I would likely discover that it led to a spike in stress-related responses such as high heart rate, mental frustration, induction of cortisol to the system, etc. Stress ruins accuracy; it is that simple. Even now, once I realize there is a problem, I immediately go to dry fire to determine whether my fundamentals are off. If the problem persists, I begin my checklist. I compare my list to NASA's preflight checklist before the launch of the space shuttle into orbit. One thing at a time, I check the fundamental aspects of the rifle, the ammunition, the ballistic solution, and the environment. I check my baselines in terms of each category. I have never encountered a problem on the range that I couldn't eventually figure out the cause of, even if it takes a couple of weeks.

You could call what I do trial and error or even simply failure. At the end of the day, it is processing information and building a checklist, and it is applicable to everything in your life from school, to skills, to relationships and interactions. I didn't explain long-range shooting in detail because I don't think it is the only thing that teaches you the ability to overcome. You can apply analysis, isolation, and solution to literally anything, but you must contain the frustration that comes with the problem. The absolute and undeniable first step is to control your feelings. My first reaction when I encounter a problem today is to solve it. My first reaction has nothing to do with my emotions or my feelings. This requires practice, and I have found that centering yourself is often the best way to think through everything you do. Every bit of information our body takes in can quickly become overwhelming. When a shooter has invested $5,000 in a rifle and scope, spent countless hours loading ammunition, and poured hundreds of dollars into training, notwithstanding the countless hours of practice, it is easy to fall prey to frustration when something doesn't go right.

What we must understand is that no matter how much investment we have made in something, failure is inevitable and is never personal. My gun doesn't fail because it doesn't like me. It fails because it is a mechanical object that I likely didn't maintain or understand well enough. With a tad more complexity, the same is true of relationships. Relationships are not easy to maintain, but if you do not apply yourself to understanding the problems and finding solutions, then you have already failed. You must maintain the tenacity to solve problems if you want to succeed. That is all it takes, but it isn't easy. It doesn't matter if you are absolutely terrible at personal finance. If you focus on analyzing your spending, isolating where you are losing money, and commit to solving that problem, you will eventually succeed at better managing your personal finances. If you take your ego out of the equation and control the inevitable rush of emotion that comes with the situations you are struggling with, you will become better at solving your problems.

More often than not we are only celebrating success. What if we actually celebrated our failures? The things I've learned throughout my life came from my failures. My failures taught me how to succeed and now I celebrate the hardest failures I've ever encountered because they taught me more than any of my success.

CONTROL

Building a solution-focused mindset begins with emotional control. It doesn't mean we should lose all emotion; rather, we should control emotion and learn to apply it wisely. Being successful requires powerful feelings, but those requirements are in how you inspire yourself. If your thinking inspires you to react out of frustration, that is exactly what will happen. If your thinking is focused on centering yourself in the moment and controlling your breathing before analyzing the situation and how you can affect change, you will do just that. Practicing the former will ensure you are consistently stressed, while practicing the latter will engage your logical brain. Practice this thousands of times over, and you will become exceptionally good at it. If you consciously interrupt the emotional choice, you will find yourself creating a paradigm shift in your emotional control. Skills require consistent, conscious thought to rebuild. You may fail the first few times, or the first few hundred or thousand times, but you *will* progress.

Constant progress is how people succeed, although that progress comes with the high cost of failing a thousand times. That is what it takes. Michael Jordan, Alex Rodriguez, Lionel Messi, and Tom Brady didn't come out of the womb as Hall of Fame athletes. Read about their rise and you will understand exactly how hard they worked, but how they also solved their problems and kept progressing their individual game while others were focused on who was watching. They had the integrity to tell themselves to do the right thing when people *weren't* watching. They practiced for themselves and not so their coaches would see them getting better. My choice was no different. I had to practice and fail hundreds of thousands of times to rebuild my mindset. If you don't have the desire to do it for yourself and your own success, then you have already failed yourself. Thinking itself is a problem that can be solved. It takes work, it takes commitment; it takes being worked on it every day of your life. If you are not working on it daily, you will not change.

Change is the only constant in this world; in our time, we have witnessed incredible change. Cell phones change how people think in a matter of minutes. Defining our ability to control our feelings is certainly no easy task. Connectivity hasn't necessarily made things any easier. Constant news, information, and communication change the way we do business, manage relationships, and learn. For all the wisdom the Internet might offer, the problems that define failure and need to be overcome are more present than ever before. Anxiety, depression, and heart disease all stem from a failure to control that which is within us, not outside of us. If you haven't learned how to change, your thinking is likely the problem. If you deal with the same failed relationships or failed work situations or can't break through a plateau in your life, you likely have not isolated the problem within yourself to solve. I can't stress how important it is to blame yourself first. That said, don't simply blame yourself and do nothing. Take action, isolate, and solve your problems. If you have not read *Extreme Ownership: How Navy SEALs Lead and Win* by Jocko Willink and Leif Babin, you are doing yourself a disservice.[6] There are many resources available to you to help renegotiate your thinking. Do not stop at this one.

It can be said that society has experienced many downfalls in recent years and even decades. I often hear people discuss what is wrong with society. I have

---

6   Willink, Jocko and Babin, Leif, *Extreme Ownership: How U.S. Navy SEALs Lead and Win.*

fallen into that trap many times myself; I can certainly call myself a hypocrite. The problem is that we see the problems and focus on those problems. It is a terribly negative way of dealing with life. It is very easy to throw stones at a problem; in fact, it is natural. The truly difficult task that must be undertaken is to research the fundamentals of the issue and generate a solution. Too often, people fall into the category of critic, which can be helpful to a point, but when an entire culture is based on critiquing rather than problem-solving, progress stagnates. I recommend taking an objective look at your day and considering how much time and energy is spent on internal and external criticism.

Lanny Bassham, and his book *With Winning in Mind*, is responsible for my conceptualization of what it means to be positive-focused.[7] There is a major tendency to focus on the problem, to the degree in fact that it dominates the space within your mind that should be focused on the solution. This falls perfectly in line with controlling emotion and feelings, in two ways. The first tendency is micro-level thinking. Individual thinking focuses on the problem, and thus we become less capable of solving critical issues. Growth comes from a wider focus, the big picture. Thinking is an individual skill that requires practice, perfect practice. Positive self-talk and rehearsal when it comes to thinking are forms of learning that are generally limited to educational curricula yet are some of the most important aspects

---

[7]   Bassham, Lanny, *With Winning in Mind*.

of Olympic gold medal-earning routines. The second tendency is societal-level thinking when it comes to dramatic problems. There is an industry focused on turning people into problem-focused individuals who then congregate in a single line of thinking: the media. You see, individual thought combined with like-minded individuals repeating consistent language, traditions, and rituals is the creation of a culture. If that culture does not include solution-focused thinking, society falls into a problem-based logic system. Growth does not branch out easily from problem-focused mindsets.

If you don't start now—if you fail to commit to reaching your potential in a positive way—you will only have yourself to blame when you don't achieve the success you desire. You can't be a millionaire without learning how to manage your finances, much as you can't be an NFL MVP without putting in more work than the other players to overcome your weaknesses. Greatness requires problem-solving. Problem-solving demands that you find the problems which will hold you back. If you don't choose to solve your problems, people will eventually stop caring about your complaints. Being a broken record doesn't solve problems—evaluation, isolation, and action solve problems. Build your foundation by renegotiating your thinking.

If this chapter helped you better understand yourself, post about it and use the hashtag (#FindASolution).

Chapter 3

BUILD A
FOUNDATION

stepped onto the plane alongside my friend. It was just another day, another flight for the many people who were standing around me. This one, however, was personally significant. On that brisk March day in 2018, I took a step toward believing in the dream of living a life I had never thought possible. My mind shuffled through the extraordinary events that had transpired to bring me to this point. Only three years before, I had worried about surviving every day, and at times, every minute. This was a morbid but true thought I'd had for over twenty years, and I had to fight the constant insecurities and urges that made me feel like a burden to those around me. My life, it seemed, had been on a knife-edge for a very long time.

I could still remember the many times I had brushed off death like it was a pesky friend I just didn't feel like talking to. Death is inevitable, but we have so much more control in our society than we are led to believe. What I hadn't known for most of my life . . . was control.

I was blinded by someone else's vision for my life, instead of creating my own. My father's choice had become my inevitability. I could not foresee any other outcome for myself than death by my own hand. I felt I was doomed to become him because I felt I *was* him. I was his son and therefore I was to relive his mistakes out of my mind's own twisted sense of the future. I was trapped within myself and unable to expose what I felt was too morbid for others to hear: my suicide. My fear left me believing no one could possibly understand what I saw and how I had mentally processed my father's death. How could anyone help me when no one around me had lost a father to suicide? I built my pessimism like castle walls around an unanswerable question: "Why did you do it?" The context wasn't as simple as my father committing suicide; he had left me after lying to me. He had unknowingly compounded my grief with guilt—or did he?

It became my own version of *Inception*: my dream within a dream, or more accurately my nightmare within a nightmare. Each moment affected the next, further heightening my castle walls around a question I could ask no one else. I had no closure; I had to live with the fact that I was never going to understand why. It was the hardest lesson I have ever had to learn in my life. I was six years old yet trying to answer questions about life that most people only ever deal with as an adult if at all. I had questions that plunged into the complexities of human emotion and mental disorders. Yet, I had grown up the instant my father pulled the trigger to end his life. In the coming months, my sorrow and pain grew into normalcy. In the days that passed after I learned of his death, my mind went into overdrive. I had unanswerable questions, I had a traumatic loss, and I had been exposed to the wrong way to deal with emotional distress. That is the recipe to bring a human being to their rock bottom. There was no glorious breakdown that allowed me to answer all my questions and deal with my problems. No, I broke every single day, while silently biding my time. I destroyed myself like my father did himself. I kept the entire swath of emotions and thoughts that simmered within me to myself.

But I made one choice that I believe my father never made: I chose to build principles to live by. I took action. Not just action, but positive action. They were principles I realistically shouldn't have needed to worry about at that age, but I built them anyway. I silently stumbled upon the solution to my own problem. It should come as no surprise that I have relatively few memories of my childhood. I don't recall why I chose to formulate these specific principles, but I imagine the idea took root after my mother exposed some details of my father's life. Details like his alcoholism, his depression, and his issues with drugs became clear in my mind. What follow are the principles I chose to implement in my life in the months after my father's suicide:

1.   I will never drink alcohol.
2.   I will never use tobacco.
3.   I will never do drugs.
4.   I will never commit suicide.

Each principle was paired with a specific understanding of my father's story. I couldn't account for his depression or his possible bipolar nature, but I learned that I could adjust my trajectory by accounting for what I *could* control. This is what would later save my life. I learned to control what I could control, and I learned this on my own. I began to let go of what I couldn't control by focusing on simply controlling my own actions. You see, I was forced to live within a box that was outside the normal box. I was alone and left to fend for myself. It was my own unconscious choice, however. I pushed the world, to include my family members, away. I had to keep my distance because of the magnitude of mental processing happening in my young brain, which I had thrust upon myself. I forced myself to blaze my own trail into my brain. My adaptation was the key that would release me.

Interactions became different for me from that point forward. They weren't just interactions; they were moments that could affect my life. I believe every moment matters. When you believe so recklessly that your father killed himself because you weren't enough for him, you change things. My guilt and my fear developed into a forward-thinking mindset. I began to listen to people intently because I couldn't bear the thought of someone else I knew taking their own life. I spoke less and listened more. My father's death taught me another rule of life that some people have a hard time learning: Ego gets in the way. Or, as Rick Rigsby once said, "Ego is the anesthesia that deadens the pain of stupidity." This is arguably one of the truest quotes I have ever encountered (check out his speech on YouTube: "Lessons from a 3rd Grade Dropout).[8] I lost my ego because I had been metaphorically hit by a truck; my ego was deadening absolutely nothing. Every second, I was in pain. And that pain lasted for almost twenty years of my life.

My struggle never manifested in my father's choices, but it certainly wasn't absent from my life. To be completely honest, the first three principles constituted the easiest rules I have ever decided to follow. I had seen firsthand what drugs, alcohol, and tobacco can do to a man, and I was having none of it. I developed an extreme personal distaste for these vices, yet I would accept it from others. But I struggled a great deal with the last principle: *I will never commit suicide.*

---

[8] Goalcast, "*The Most Inspiring Speech: The Wisdom of a Third Grade Dropout Will Change Your Life | Rick Rigsby,*" 5 October 2017, (10:21), https://youtu.be/Bg_Q7KYWG1g

On a spring day in 2015, almost twenty years after my father's death, I hit my rock bottom. Until that day, my rebuilt ego had gotten in my way. On that day, I wholeheartedly believed that I was holding people back and causing them hurt, and I was contemplating following my father to the grave. It defied logic, as anyone who knew me at the time would likely agree that I wasn't holding back or harming anyone. Regardless, another law of life is that someone's perspective is their reality.

My perspective was my reality. I put a gun to my head because I felt a sense of false righteousness. It was not my pride that brought me to my knees; it was something else entirely. My father, my mother told me while I was in Afghanistan, had set up an insurance policy that passed the initial one-year suicide clause a few weeks prior to his death. Many people consider suicide is selfish, but in my eyes my father was as selfless as one could possibly be. My father, an alcoholic, who was suffering from depression and was occasionally abusive and immensely insecure, thought he had found a way to rid us of his perception of reality while also providing for us. He was ending his negative influence on his family and leaving us with his version of support. Suicide may be as selfish as society tends to believe, but it isn't always as selfish as it might seem. Did my father make the right choice or the wrong choice? Honestly, that isn't for us to decide.

In my own emotional wave of thinking, I put the muzzle of my loaded Glock 34 directly below my ear. As morose as it sounds, I wanted to make sure I hit my medulla oblongata; it is the one place that functions as a guaranteed shutoff switch for the body. It completely negates any muscle contraction upon death and leaves the muscles relaxed. I believed so clearly that I was about to end the negative effects I was having on my family and friends; I was making the world a better place. I felt the cold metal of my Glock barrel when it touched my skin, which instantly made me take a deep breath through my tearful sobs. It was like stepping into a pool for the first time. With one round in the chamber, I pulled every ounce as I sobbed on the floor of my mother's hallway, saving one. In that instant, I held myself to the only principle that truly mattered. Even thinking of that moment induces the same sadness I sensed when I thought of how my father must have felt. What stayed my hand was a realization of my own ignorance. In that moment, I realized that my life had been a self-fulfilling prophecy. I had become what I feared most, and I had allowed my emotion to trump my logic. And I fell that day. I fell *hard* that day. I was a grown man crying on the floor with a loaded gun in his hand and no awareness of whether he was going to survive the next few moments. It still baffles me that I had enough control to hold myself back.

I say it baffles me, yet I know the answer. We are hard-wired to survive. Remember, our amygdala makes choices for us a split second before our Neo-Cortex. Our bodies choose life even when our minds wish for death. I learned this lesson a few years before my own battle with suicide while I was in Afghanistan on my first deployment. Even up until then, I had wished for death every day since my father had killed himself . . . sixteen years later. As my squad conducted a normal route recon of a road we hadn't been down before, we encountered something peculiar. It wasn't something we saw or heard; it was something we felt. We, not just I, each felt a heavy feeling that we couldn't explain as we made our turn north onto a road that could barely be classified as gravel. The massive gouges and bumps in the road weren't the uncomfortable part as we stared into the blackness of the night. All three of us stopped instantly and almost simultaneously expressed our revulsion for where we were going. We made a decision that night that saved our lives.

We didn't know it until we returned to our base. In the night, we were unable to see what was in front of our MRAP. When we returned to base, we were told that two men were seen planting an IED around 400 yards down that dark road. That feeling in the pit of your stomach doesn't come from nowhere. I believe our bodies recognize far more than our mind ever will. Our actions that day saved us from death and yet I still wished for it every single day. The profoundness of that moment has stuck with me. The mind may wish for death but the power our bodies have to survive is so difficult to overcome. To choose suicide requires such deep inner conflict, guilt, or shame that we override our body's survival response.

My trial was ongoing, with nineteen years of self-destruction being realized in my single greatest moment of weakness. It was not a glorious moment of self-realization of everything I now know. No, it was the beginning: a launchpad for the man I was to become. I had learned my laws intuitively and found my own answer to that unanswerable question. I didn't need to conform to someone else's perspective to find my way. The same way I fell apart almost twenty years before was the way I was going to put myself back together. Another law of life was borne in that moment: You cannot undo years of self-destruction in a single moment. I had always believed that my father was a selfish man, because that was how people explained and rationalized suicide to me. I was inundated with a social response to a problem that had never been solved. My struggle changed my perception of suicide; it changed my perception of my father. In the coming years, I learned to respect him because I empathize with him and found my path to closure. I needed to process his death in a positive way to overcome it, regardless of how it was viewed.

You see, I followed him to the gates, but I didn't walk through. I came as close to death as any man has ever come. Part of me thought of myself as a coward for not following through that day, but I soon learned otherwise. Power lies in our ability to stand against the easy choice. I chose the hard right over the easy wrong. I had to begin the arduous process of renegotiating my repetitious thought process. What I learned that day brought me the clarity I needed to renegotiate how I understood my story. Once I understood, I could isolate the problem and change. My reaction to emotional stress was cyclical, which consistently resulted in emotional breakdowns. I refused to accept my thought process as broken, however. My ego led me down the same path my father had walked long before me. I had to hit rock bottom to fully understand that my ego was the problem. Thinking negatively almost killed me. Re-defining my thoughts brought me to become both realistic and positive.

There was just one step I needed to take before I could assure myself that I was headed in the right direction. I had to tell the people closest to me that I was at rock bottom. At the time of my breakdown, I was alone. I had incredibly close friends, who knew nothing about my daily struggle with suicide. My struggle was a personal hell; it was my deepest, darkest secret. I told no one for several days. Honestly, I had told no one about the thoughts that had tormented me my entire life. So, I made a plan to own my problems and my weaknesses by telling the people I found easiest to talk to: my best friends Chris and Carey. I shared with Carey first, his response, with hindsight, is:

> I was a little shocked. But I was more shocked you told me. I knew you had your battles, and it didn't surprise me that you had contemplated it. What did surprise me was how close you came to actually

> doing it. And that you were confiding in
> me at that moment. I had always thought
> of you as an impenetrable force and for
> the first time I saw your vulnerabilities,
> but it was amazing the amount of respect
> I gained for you in that moment.

Carey's response showed me the social implications of silence. People saw my father as an 'impenetrable force' just as my friends and family saw me. I've always been a good actor, that's why people didn't know. Suicidal ideation creates the best actors in the world, but it also takes them too early.

I followed telling my friends by sharing with the people I knew I would find most difficult: my sister and mother. My mother was the rock in the phrase, "Between a rock and a hard place." An intelligent and focused woman, my mother never seemed to know that defeat was possible, or at least she hid it as well as I did. She looked at people with respect and expected it in return. She had an inextinguishable fire, and her ferocity and tenacity carried over to her children.

I learned my lessons from my mother. I took responsibility for my problems and owned my weaknesses. I took my time to understand and comprehend my problem. Instead of blaming my father, I began to blame myself first, much as I would do with shooting. Those three days that I waited to tell my friends and family brought me clarity. I forced myself to let go of the burden of blaming my father and focused on solving myself.

I remember sitting down at the counter of my mom's house. She was standing across from me, as I collected myself by looking out the window to the birds playing on the porch. I knew nothing was going to stop the flood of emotions that was about to swell within me. Before I could speak, I began to cry as I handed her a letter that explained what happened. It was several minutes before I spoke softly and slowly about what I had done a few days prior. Every word I spoke released immense weight from my soul; tears fell from my eyes as if someone had turned on a faucet. I watched my mother cry as she listened to her son tell her how close he had come to letting go. Nothing, absolutely nothing, can prepare you to tell your mother that kind of news. It was and will likely always be the most difficult conversation of my life. It was also the most necessary.

I fought myself for almost twenty years. I looked to death because I was never taught how to live. My pain and suffering became a self-fulfilling prophecy. I pitied myself for what I had been through, yet I never spoke to myself about the strength it took to get through it all. I spoke to others, but I often played a strong character. I'd be a great actor, given the chance; I've been practicing all my life. It took twenty years to learn that lying to everyone and faking it was not going to solve my problems. Only I could solve my problems, and no matter how many lies I told people, my problems would only become bigger. It was the thought of how I affected others that made the difference. I began to embody the most important word in the human language: empathy.

Empathy changed my life. Sadly, I didn't begin to understand the definition of the word until after my battle. Language is simply a way of communicating; true understanding comes in many forms of learning. With every passing day I was taught empathy by my mother, my sister, and the few others I had allowed into the darkness of my mind. Empathy is listening to understand. It is the ability to accept another person's feelings and to disregard any disrespect they may present. You must be able to put yourself in their shoes and not take anything personally; that is empathy. Empathy doesn't forgive people for wrongdoing. That isn't the point. Empathy is a reminder that they have someone who is willing to understand them, yet who has no expectations. No matter the reason, there is no excuse for doing the wrong thing. You must answer for your mistakes, but that doesn't mean you have to do it alone. Too many believe no one can understand them but the reality is more likely the fear of or inability to express feelings.

Empathy has curative and trust-building powers. Those who are openly willing to feel what you feel become trusted. To share vulnerabilities is among the many reasons for mankind's separation from nature. Nature is dependent on the survival of those who continuously adapt to their environment by maximizing their strengths. Weakness rarely survives for long outside the realm of society. Humanity survives because societies protect themselves from their weaknesses by working together. Unity is an important trait within society, one that has dramatic effects on human lives. Tight networks that remain supportive become efficient and top performing. When empathy is a focal point of the team, people focus on being supportive of one another.

My foundation was built upon empathy. This book was written to foster the world's empathy through my sharing of my story. I created myself by following the principles I am offering you. My foundation is responsible for my goals. I started out simply surviving. My goal is now centered on helping others survive their most difficult moments. Not just survive, though; my goal is to help people understand that every difficult moment has given them extraordinary strength. The moments you spend struggling, crying, wincing, and failing are your greatest moments of strength. We rarely define strength this way because it isn't heroic and pretty. Now is the time for you to transform your perception of strength. The world needs people to stand up, look forward, and solve the problems facing us. We need a society that will lean into the storm. You don't build success without a foundation, whether personal or societal.

Principles are the beginning of a foundation. You can dream and then achieve. You can find happiness beyond the hardest and most traumatic moments in life. Rome wasn't built in a day. If you want to find happiness, if you want to be something, if you want to become somebody, it may take weeks, months, years, and, as in my case, decades to find your way. The law is this: If you truly want it, wake up every day, no matter how hard it is, and do the work. Never quit fighting for what you want. If you need to learn more, learn more. If you need more connections, network. If you need help, ask for it. But every single day of your life, be relentless. Wake up and choose to act.

Every successful foundation needs—let me repeat, *needs*—the determination to never give up. The audacity to never quit, regardless of what people tell you, is necessary for greatness. Success is not going to wait for you to sleep in; it prospers from your hard work and effort. If you never stop putting in effort and continue to push forward, then nothing will stop your progress. Be tenacious and don't take no for an answer. No is an answer that will either expose your weaknesses or your strengths. If you choose to accept it as an answer, you will see nothing but weakness. If you choose to keep going regardless, you will have strength. The mystique behind "no" is the judgment. Everyone will judge you. We are judgmental creatures. Learn to stop caring what other people think. Most who judge you will likely never have done what you are attempting to do, so they won't and can't possibly understand. The haters will often trash talk because they are struggling. The ones who support you are the ones you need to keep around.

You see, success is a system. Or, as Lanny Bassham says, it is a process. If you don't build it right, it becomes harder for you to achieve. Success is similar to life itself, in that life on Earth grows in certain environmental conditions. Success grows the same way. It is fostered by the environment around it. To build success, the various pieces, people, attitudes, work ethics, mindsets—everything—needs to fit together. The primordial soup of success is multi-dimensional and boasts many intrinsic characteristics.

Before I continue, I must address how I define my success and at what points in my life that definition changed. You see, success is fluid. Success can change at any moment because of perspective and self-image. My success is not the commonly imagined wealth evident in a big house, fancy cars, and large portfolio. My success is based on character development, mindset building, and logical thinking. Confidence in who you are is an achievable success. Believing in yourself and in your ability to be content with what you have can make anyone rich. Success can literally be whatever you want it to be. For me, there was a time in my life that surviving meant I was succeeding.

I define my success by how I think. Years passed during which I was hiding a suicidal mindset. I constantly lied to my closest friends and my loved ones. I couldn't escape myself as I suffered in the only way I knew how: within. Today, I have built a successful mindset. I continue to hold to my principles and the promises I made to myself. Now, I measure my success on a different path; a path toward helping others who do not have the courage to tell anyone they are fighting the urge to follow death's calling. Today, my success is the fulfillment I find in helping others. Teaching people the path to a better life is my passion, and I follow it every single day. I don't care if this book nets me no money for all my work, so long as it keeps one person from taking their life. My goal is for you to defy your darkness.

Don't expect anything from anyone beyond the fact that they will affect you. Expectations will destroy your foundations. Expectations are for you and your achievements alone. The second you start expecting things for the work you do is the moment you begin to lose sight of why you are doing the work. Don't ever let yourself lose sight of your vision. Vision is what maintains your foundation. Vision defines your principles. Your ability to conceive your future is how you shape your life. Your success is what you see for yourself; that is vision. Foundations are built so that the weight of success may stand the test of time.

Build yourself a foundation that delivers exactly what you want. Write down your vision and remind yourself why you are working through all the difficulties you face. Find comfort in the uncomfortable moments in life. Learn from them and adapt to everything around you. Be tenacious. Be relentless. Be yourself. Be undeniably you.

If this chapter struck a chord in your heart, post about it and #DefytheDarkness.

Chapter 4

INVEST IN UNDERSTANDING WHY

"Why?" is the most influential question one can ask. Fundamental knowledge is built upon why things are the way they are. To understand who you are, you must ask yourself *why?* This question helps you begin to understand the fundamentals of yourself. Investing in your mind is the only investment that cannot be taken from you. Everything else can be gone in an instant. You can lose all your money in an economic downturn. You can lose your business due to a lawsuit. You can lose your job for any number of reasons. Friends walk away due to misunderstandings and disagreements. Even family isn't safe, because anyone can die at any time. You will lose so much throughout your life. Yet, no one can take away your experience, knowledge, and character. Understanding why you are the way you are will bring you clarity when you begin to consider why you do things. If you want to be happy, be successful, be your best, you must understand why you are continuing. *Why* is the key to unlocking your passion for life.

But what is passion? It is easy to recognize passion in the people we encounter, but what does it really mean? I consider passion the emotional connection that drives us toward identifying the reasons why we choose to act. The key word in that definition is "why," and is the focus of this chapter. Passion is directly related to why you do what you do. Every single day, the choices you make are affected by your defining principles and your emotions. I will address two important understandings of *why*: first, the fundamental understanding that is only uncovered by asking the question, "Why;" and second, the concept of passion. My obsession with *why* began with my father. I was forced to face the question head-on as I sought an answer to why he killed himself. I was on my own. No one could help me, least of all him.

While I was growing up, *why* became an obsession due to the nature of my father's choice. The problem with suicide is that there is never a clear picture of why that person decides to end their life. Even leaving a note doesn't always communicate the *why* with clarity. In my father's case, we had no note. We had no closure, no reason, no idea why. All we could do was speculate as to the *why*. In that vacuum, my mother shared with me the conditions of his situation and left me to decide his reasons *why*. She only told me that he was an alcoholic, depressed, potentially bipolar, and occasionally tried drugs like cocaine. I was six years old and knew nothing about any of it. All I could truly comprehend was the simple fact that my father had left me, but I had no clue as to why. That curiosity would mold and shape me every day of my life. It terrorized my mind for years, yet it also helped me adapt to learn quickly.

As I learned throughout school, I became curious about why and how things worked. I could work my way through complex things because I looked deeper than other people did. I forced levels of understanding beyond what public school offered. I wasn't the smartest, but after everything I had been through, I was built to learn. I was built to learn because it was what I chose. Every situation I walked into was one that could teach me about this world that had so thoroughly wrecked my life. Who was I to deserve what happened and continued to happen to me?

School brought me knowledge; it helped me develop my mind, but it also hurt me. After my father's death, I became very shy and introverted. I didn't know how to talk to other kids. Being as traumatized as I was by my father's death left me confused and shaken. I couldn't relate well to the kids who were enjoying their lives. At school, I would focus on every word the teacher said; it was often the only way to get my mind off my father. When I wasn't being taught, I would read books about war. I remember being fascinated by war after my mother met her boyfriend a few years after my father's death. He was in the Navy during the Vietnam War and was very knowledgeable on the subject. He had movies and books on everything from warplanes to World War II. To this day, I still remember watching every one of those videos over and over again. I was a sponge.

The military became a prospect for me when I began feeling that I needed to atone for what my father had chosen to do. In the beginning of high school, I learned that it was a sin to commit suicide, and how in Christianity it meant going to hell. At the time, I was struggling with my own views of religion and whether to believe in a higher power or cast out the idea entirely. It was this simple concept that drove me to the military, even if later it didn't matter to me. It was the inception of my father. The military became a way for me to return my family name to honor after my dad committed suicide. Sound crazy? It was. I made a major decision about my future because I believed I needed to make my name look better, and I didn't care whether I lived or died. I put my life on the line for the simple idea of how I thought people judged me and my family. In fact, in a way I hoped for death. I joined the infantry hoping that I would give my life and earn my fictive place in our family.

It was these early decisions that I would later have to face head-on.

I joined the Wisconsin Army National Guard in January of 2008, a couple of weeks before my eighteenth birthday. My mom knew I had made up my mind and signed off on the paperwork to let her only boy join the infantry. By the end of July, I was sweating out my struggle in the woods and swamps of Fort Benning, Georgia. My Infantry Basic Combat Training lasted approximately sixteen weeks and forced me to focus on learning quickly or paying the consequences. Infantry, more than any other job, teaches a cruel lesson: it isn't about you. You are only as good as your weakest link; when that link fails in basic, everyone pays for it. You either learn to work together or you get really strong together. Drill sergeants search for any reason to punish the group for one person's failure, and they found those failures more often than we liked.

You learn a lot about society in the infantry. The barriers against women in combat arms hadn't fallen at that time, of course; but the military has, for the most part, been on the leading edge of social unity. I had various soldiers of different races, ethnicities, and backgrounds in my basic training. We were all equally worthless until we earned the respect of the group. The beauty of basic training is the simple idea that it's not about you. If you don't do what you need to do, people can die. That is war. You can be the very best and still die. Everyone must sacrifice for the safety of the group. No one is above that;

each person must pay the same dues. For many of us, it was a raw and unrelenting lesson.

To summarize what it means to be in the infantry, many years ago I came across a write-up by an anonymous author that speaks everything I would like to say about being infantry. I've kept this for years because it truly characterizes who we are as a group. Some fit better than others, and those who don't quite fit often end up making the decision to leave. "The Infantryman's Arrogance" is the aptly named title of this excerpt. I don't know the author of this work, but I would gladly give credit to them if I ever found out.

The Infantryman's Arrogance

Infantry have a pride and arrogance that most Americans don't understand and don't like. Even soldiers who aren't infantry don't understand. The pride doesn't exist because we have a job that's physically impressive. It certainly doesn't exist because it takes a higher level of intelligence to perform our duties. It's sad and I hate to admit it, but any college student or high school grad can physically do what we do. It's not THAT demanding and doesn't take a physical anomaly. Nobody will ever be able to compare us to professional athletes or fitness models. And it doesn't take a very high IQ to read off serial numbers, pack bags according to a packing list, or know that incoming bullets have the right of way.

The pride of the infantryman comes not from knowing that he's doing a job that others can't, but that he's doing a job that others simply won't. Many infantrymen haven't seen a lot of combat. While that may sound ideal to the civilian or non-infantry soldier, it pains the grunt. We signed up to spit in the face of danger. To walk the line between life and death and live to do it again - or not. To come to terms with our own mortality and let others try to take our life instead of yours. We have raised our hands and said, 'Take me, America. I am willing to kill for you. I am willing to sacrifice my limbs for you. I will come back to America scarred and disfigured for you. I will be the first to die for you.'

That's why the infantryman carries himself with pride and arrogance. He's aware that America has lost respect for him. To many he's a bloodthirsty animal. To others he's too uneducated and stupid to get a regular job or go to college. Only he knows the truth. While there are few in America who claim to have respect for him, the infantry man returns from war with less fanfare than a first down in a high school football game. Yes, people hang up their 'Support the Troops' ribbons and on occasion thank us for our service. But in their eyes the infantryman can detect pity and shame; not respect. Consider this: How excited would you be to meet the average infantryman? Now compare that with how excited you'd be to meet a famous actor or professional sports player and you will find that you, too, are guilty of placing the wrong people on a pedestal. You wouldn't be able to tell me how many soldiers died in the war last month, but you'd damn sure be able to tell me if one of the actors from Twilight died.

Yet the infantryman doesn't complain about that. He continues to do his job; to volunteer his life for you, all while being paid less in four years than Tom Brady makes in one game.

It's a job most Americans don't understand, don't envy, and don't respect. That is why we have pride for the infantry."[9]

It is rare that people think of the infantry. People think of police officers and firefighters, because they truly have dangerous jobs; but how often do you see something dedicated to supporting infantry? They make movies

---

[9]   Knottie, *"The Infantrymen's Arrogance,"* Knottie's Niche, 16 November 2011, https://knottiesniche.com/2011/11/16/the-infantrymens-arrogance/ 20 September 2020.

about us but few would know how to tell the difference between us and other soldiers. Infantrymen are often thought of as loud, obnoxious, uneducated, and bred to enact violence upon the very same people in other nations' armies. I have seen nothing but silent professionals who struggle with back issues, knee issues, PTSD, traumatic brain injuries, and identity issues, yet who try to stay in the only brotherhood that mattered to them. White, black, Latino, Asian, Native American; it doesn't matter, because we are a brotherhood that shares the most important quality any group can possess: choice. We all chose the nation over ourselves.

The infantry ignited the fire that built my *why* over the years. My capacity for empathy combined with the absolute need to work for the good of the group were in perfect alignment. The reason I act is to better the team, the squad, the group, or the society. It no longer matters who it is—my goal is to build a better world, and I know that starts with how people think of themselves. I knew from the outset that I was going to have to be strong. There are so many people in the world who struggle to survive, who think of themselves as lower than they really are, or who lack the confidence to choose to live. I didn't become strong because of the infantry. I was strong long before I joined the Army, I just didn't know it. People seem to have this idea that standing stoically against the storm is the only way you can be strong. That's an idealistic look at an emotion that is nothing more than a choice. Strength comes from within. It is a choice to keep going. Whether or not you feel sadness, pain, hatred, or anything else along with your strength doesn't change the fact that you kept going. Survival is strength.

Infantry Basic Training was my beginning. It revealed my strength and eventually ignited my passion. Up until that point, my life didn't reveal many opportunities for me to enjoy myself. Life as an infantryman brought me in contact with two things that would eventually make major contributions to my character: firearms and leadership. It may seem like an odd pairing, but it doesn't matter what builds character as long as something does. Both firearms and leadership revealed to me different ways to be passionate and brought me closer to understanding why I decided to act.

Following basic training, I bought my first rifle, a Remington 700 with a heavy barrel. It was this very rifle that would ultimately help me define my life. The rifle, this tool, brought me much reflection over the years, which remains with me to this day. It will always be the only firearm I never give up. I came out of basic training a fundamentally above-average shooter. I was nothing special, but I grew very fond of the idea that I might be capable of perfecting my skill. This rifle was my way of becoming better. So, in the winter of 2008, I began my quest to perfect the skill of shooting.

I still remember reading and researching and looking up every shooting article I could find. I would read anything I could get my hands on. This tenacious learning style would later become useful when I fell in love with overcoming myself. I began with the fundamentals of marksmanship, but soon found myself funneled toward reading on the science of ballistics. You see, the fundamentals of marksmanship are simply the bare minimum. They are the necessary requirements to perform the process. Understanding ballistics, optics, and the environment is where the real magic happens. You start these journeys through life expecting to discover an easy path, but skills are never easily mastered. There is always more depth, no matter how good you are. The best can always be better—there is always perfection.

For the first year, I shot on a friend's farm near Green Bay, Wisconsin. It was only about 300 yards, but it offered me a chance to perfect my fundamentals. Weather never mattered to me. I would go out in that muddy field in the 95-degree heat of muggy summer or in the freezing, bitter cold of winter. It takes true dedication to get out of the car during a Wisconsin winter, let alone shoot for hours in the elements. That is exactly what I was: dedicated. I would shoot in the prone; lying in snow and ice for hours takes a certain level of passion. It never mattered to me, however. My dedication is built upon passion, and that passion doesn't give a damn about my comfort. That is what always made the difference in my life. It was the times when I knew my comfort was not a priority that real growth happened.

I still remember setting up the cardboard target with a couple of pieces of firewood, walking back to the gun, sending three rounds, and walking back to check the target. What they don't tell you about shooting is how much walking is involved. To check the target, I would walk 600 yards, often only to be disappointed that the shot wasn't acceptable. I would think through each shot I took as I walked down to the target, then think about what I could do better as I walked back. The only way I could improve was to think through how I could do better, but I was always punching above my weight. I was still thinking very one-dimensionally as I broke those shots when I first started.

The sheer number of things that can go wrong when shooting is immense. When you begin adding distance, those variables only increase. The gun itself is a mechanical object. It can fail. Action screws can loosen from recoil, which makes shots inconsistent. Scope mounts and bases can become loose, meaning the optic and the gun will be looking at two different places from shot to shot. Barrels can become too fouled up with debris, thereby slowing the bullet, which will change the trajectory and make shots inconsistent. The stock of the firearm itself may not be rigid enough to control vibration, which allows the barrel to flex too much, which creates wide shot groups. The bolt of a bolt-action rifle can break. Scopes can break. Even the most consistent action out there can fail. These failures often have nothing to do with the shooter, but they do affect the performance of that shooter. How do you deal with these failures that have nothing to do with you?

Everything I've listed above has happened to me. The concept circles back to Chapter 1 in which you learned to analyze and understand the problem before finding a solution. As a competitive shooter, I've watched shooters fall apart when things didn't go their way. I've also watched champion shooters solve the very same problem and go on to win the competition. Two people dealing with the same problem can bring about dramatically different results. The first person may look at the firearm and blame it or its manufacturer, feeling disappointment, frustration, and anger toward an object that doesn't give a damn what they feel. The second person may analyze whether they have seen this problem before, whether they have the ability or the tools to solve the issue, and what action they can take. The second person would likely recognize the very same stress the first person feels, but they would choose to focus on the challenge of solving the problem. What is the difference?

The second person has invested in looking deeper than just feelings and emotions. In the case of my example, that requires research and understanding of the function and fundamentals of the firearm. They ask the necessary questions: How does that firearm work? Why does it work this way or that? Half of my shooting experience comes from the military, and this difference was never more apparent than between new soldiers and experienced Noncommissioned Officers (NCOs). A new soldier has likely never been exposed to how an M4 or M16 works. They often don't get the explanation of how a gas-impingement system functions. That is a failure of the military machine, but it also represents a success. The military trains actions that offer the most common solutions, but it trains that action without fostering the knowledge of how it works. The military system offers a way to train the most soldiers most successfully. Quantity over quality. Everyone will walk away from Basic Combat Training understanding the minimum reactions to their most common problems. This, unfortunately, doesn't build the second person in our example. Teaching people an action without explaining function doesn't cultivate critical thinking.

Critical thinking and adaptation come from understanding function, understanding why things are the way they are, and how they work in context. Confucius said, "By three methods we may learn: First, by reflection, which is noblest; Second, by imitation, which is easiest; and third by experience, which is bitterest." The military, at its basic level, teaches imitation, which is easiest. When a person understands how things work, they often begin to recognize when things are beginning to fail—at times, before they actually do. I mostly learned how to shoot by experience, and eventually began to introduce reflection. I didn't begin with understanding how firearms functioned. I learned by imitation, but as soon as I was learning on my own, I encountered issues the Army didn't prepare me for. Sometimes, there is no guidebook for what to do. There are going to be moments in your life when you are alone and afraid, and it will fall upon you to solve your own problem. You must learn by failing, and then you must analyze why you failed and how you can succeed within the system or the environment.

Shooting, like any skill, requires practice and experience to bring to bear the full depth of what can happen. Each fundamental must become muscle memory to be efficient. Muscle memory/reflex memory simply enhances the link between the mind and the muscle and increases the speed of the synapses' firing. For my quest, it came with experience. I focused so much on the plain and boring fundamentals by conducting hours and hours of dry-fire training. Dry-fire training is taking a shot without any ammunition in the firearm. A perfect dry-fire involves nothing that moves but the trigger. The sights stay on target and your body remains rigid, as if you are made of stone. The only movement permitted comes from the few muscles controlling the trigger. I taught myself how to shoot pistol by focusing on dry-fire; to the point, in fact, that I began teaching experienced instructors innovative ways to remind themselves to look at their own fundamentals. My skill was derived by focusing on how I could functionally change how I put force on the firearm. I analyzed every force imparted by the fundamentals and how they individually affected my shooting. Every session became a new learning experience in which I challenged myself to achieve a new level of understanding of my function as well as of the firearm's function. I attempted to reach a goal, failed, then learned a new lesson because I added an important component to my sessions. I would stop when I recognized I was too frustrated to learn.

The incorporation of minimizing my emotional frustration that I put into the process helped me grow, because I only did it when it was enjoyable. My passion drove me to succeed. Don't get me wrong: I failed many times. I remember sending two-dollar rounds downrange with my Christensen Arms 300 Winchester Magnum that I had just bought and only achieving two-inch groups at 100 yards, even though the manufacturer guaranteed one-inch groups. I dry-fired hundreds of rounds between the forty rounds I sent downrange, achieving the same result. I broke down my fundamentals to the point that I knew the issue couldn't be me. Finally, I blamed my gun. I checked my optic; nothing was wrong. Everything was tight and tracking well. My bore wasn't excessively fouled. I was perplexed. I even took my muzzle brake off, thinking the bullet could be striking the muzzle brake when it left the barrel. It wasn't that, either and I was becoming visibly frustrated. Finally, after a short pause and google open on my phone, I pulled out my Allen wrenches and checked the action screws that hold the stock to the barrel and action. It turns out that the brand-new rifle had begun to loosen the action screws from the heavy recoil from the 300 Win. Mag. That experience taught me how frustration only makes problem-solving more difficult. At the end of the day, don't let yourself get frustrated at inanimate objects—they aren't going to listen to you.

I learned how to shoot because I forced myself to experience the process, and I held myself accountable to that process. I teach people how to shoot, not simply by imitation, but by comprehension and understanding of the process. When I teach a class, people walk out understanding the function of what I just taught them, to the point that they can teach themselves how to overcome problems. Some might say you won't make money by teaching people how to teach themselves. To that I say, "Good." My goal is and always will be to help others build themselves. My passion is teaching people to overcome, not to make money. The day I stop prioritizing people over money is the day I die. There will be days that I have to prioritize money, but only so I can take care of those I love, which circles back to people. Following your passion does not mean you make yourself financially rich; it means you make yourself rich in character. It doesn't mean you can't get rich but understand that money won't solve problems that were meant for thought. Money can become just as frustrating as anything else in your life. Ultimately, it becomes far more difficult to grow when your frustration leads you to believe that you *aren't* a part of the problem. That is where ego comes in. It was Rick Rigsby who said, "Ego is the anesthesia that deadens the pain of stupidity." Learn to love failing as a part of what you're passionate about, because it is inevitable. It is where true growth originates.

If you love something in your life, your actions lead you to make it a focus. Love is action by definition.

Passion, as I have said, is the emotional connection that drives us to the reason we choose to act. Love comes from the dedication to choosing to act. That means your reasons for action are even deeper than love. There is something more fundamental than love—and that is your *why*. Humans have the ability to empower memories that can only be compared to nature through pain. We empower our memories to become the reasons for our actions. Losing a parent by suicide makes a child three times more likely to commit suicide themselves, while losing a parent regardless of cause increases a child's risk of committing a violent crime.[10] Children connect and empower their memories to action, and they will often act in self-destructive ways when faced with tragedy. That is, until they begin to understand their own strength. Why we succeed is no different: we empower the memories of that which inspires us.

My father exemplifies both sides of this concept. On the one hand, I nearly committed suicide because of the very nature of his death. I idolized his end and believed so confidently that I was exactly like my father that it nearly cost me my life. And yet, my life transformed when I began to realize precisely what my father's choice did to everyone in his life, including myself. For the first

---

[10] *Children Who Lose a Parent to Suicide More Likely to Die the Same Way.* Johns Hopkins Medicine. 21 April 2010. <https://www.hopkinsmedicine.org/news/media/releases/children_who_lose_a_parent_to_suicide_more_likely_to_die_the_same_way#:~:text=In%20the%20United%20States%2C%20each,to%20suicide%2C%20the%20researchers%20estimate.>

time, my choices brought me a better understanding of why my father had made his choice. I changed in that moment: By empowering those same memories that used to anger me, I saw the pain I had endured throughout the years as strength. I transformed my self-destruction like the phoenix rising from the ashes. My opportunity had always been within me, waiting for me to shed my burdens and truly understand why I needed to survive. You see, my life was built in the fires of my hell. Only I can help people in my way, because no one has seen what I have seen in my life. You are no different. Your *why* is worth investing in.

We empower our thoughts, our memories, our ideals, and our principles to build our character unlike any other life form on our planet. It is what you choose to empower that creates your character. Invest in understanding why you are here, in this moment. Evaluate the people around you, your environment, your experiences, and the time you've been given. Discover what you are passionate about, what you choose, and why you love it. Negotiate how you view your life to empower the best parts of your character. Invest in determining the *why* within your world and the how of your future, and you will unearth the reasons you choose to act.

Chapter 5

PRACTICE LOVE AND EMPATHY

Have you ever tried to define the word "love"? Something from *The Notebook* or another romantic movie probably comes to mind, something that has inspired your own idea of love. We are truly in a romantic age, in that love is the notion that defines relationships. The interesting thing about love is that our definitions don't seem to actually be consistent with what it takes to *love*. By this, I mean no real emotional example of love, other than passion or desire, truly exists within our culture. Love is a tenured term that seems to imply some sort of contractual obligation that one should feel a number of positive emotions toward someone else. We say we fall in love but just as easily seem to fall out of love.

Maybe we are lying to ourselves. Or maybe we just lack a complete understanding of love. So, let me discuss how I learned about love; it is the foundation of this chapter.

My mother taught me long ago that love is simply action. You do for the ones you love, because love requires action. With years under my belt, I have come to understand love as a bit more complex, although action is truly the core fundamental. Love, to be true love, must be action without expectation, if it isn't to cease being love. I believe love is the kind of word that describes why a person would sacrifice everything. If love becomes action with expectation ("You must do this because I love you"), then love becomes power, and power taints relationships. Love itself demands respect but does not imply expectations. People who give to others without expecting anything in return are often well-respected; Mother Theresa and the Dalai Lama are two such examples. By definition, love does not demand your expectations.

My definition of love is more complex than just giving without expectations, however. You can give a dollar to a homeless person without loving them or expecting anything in return. With love, there is a sense of connection that must be made, as well as a depth to that connection. To complete my definition, love refers to a relationship built with deep connection based on giving without expectations. Relationships are built upon shared experiences, thoughts, and connections, over time. It is within the context of the relationship where the expectations should be understood, *not* the action of love.

The simple expectations of most relationships are things like faithfulness and supportiveness but every person has their own ideas of what is right and wrong whether that is clearly expressed or not. It takes two minds acting without expectation to develop a lifetime of love. People rarely remain entirely the same from the day they are born to the day they die. Change is a guarantee, which means any expectation placed upon someone at twenty years old is not practical when they are seventy. Love is action, but love must be flexible. Somewhere along the way, people tend to forget that the depth of their connection can only be maintained by empathy and understanding, which takes hard work, patience, and ultimately sacrifice. It is the idea of giving these things without expectation that solidifies the connection.

To me, the friendships and relationships that I have built were created based on my definition of love. Love is a deep connection that becomes a relationship built on this simple idea of giving without expectations. Giving without expectations requires the sacrifice of something. Whether it is time, money, pride, emotions, etc., giving without expectations induces some form of sacrifice. Being a good friend often requires you to sacrifice your time and emotions, for example when you console a friend going through a break-up or mourning a family death. There is no written requirement that you have to help, but good friends know that to remain loving friends, they will sacrifice. It is about doing what is right and what helps others. That is integrity.

What is important to understand is that there is no relationship, friendship, or even marriage that will be perfectly equitable. In many of my own friendships, I offer far more emotional support than I receive. There is a vast difference in context. My life has been plagued by events that have taught me important lessons far before my friends experienced them. It's not that I am a better person; I was simply better equipped sooner. This holds for many aspects of the relationship. Some friends will have more money, others have emotional control, and some will have access to the things you enjoy doing. What matters is that you learn to give and sacrifice yourself for others. Understand that whatever you choose to lend, give, or offer may not be returned. Giving—whether in the form of time, money, or wisdom, etc.—does not enable you to stand as a gatekeeper over another. What you give is not a representation of what you will get in return. You should not expect anything in return.

What you get in return is not for you to decide. There are almost 8 billion people in the world who are all making choices in their own self-interest. Expecting people to make you the priority is futile, when many people are struggling to meet their own needs. I was fortunate to have a mother who held me accountable to work and who made me earn what I wanted. I wasn't given anything in life; I earned it. I learned to love earning my place, because it allowed me to build something of my own: a reputation. If there is a talent I possess, it is understanding people's observations. I know what is necessary to keep a good reputation, but I also know what it's like to come back from nothing. I know this because I don't act—I *do*. I do everything that is necessary, whether I like it or not. That is leadership. Good reputations fall apart when they aren't backed by consistent integrity.

I am willing to do the work that others delegate or scoff at because I know something they don't: Every action taken, every word spoken, and everything a person turns down is recorded in the minds of others around them. People watch you when you're coming up, but they'll watch even closer when you're on top. Some people don't clean the bathroom at work and will gladly delegate the task to someone in a subordinate role. What I know is that actions will be remembered. When I lead, I'm in the trenches or I'm at least willing to step down from my position's pedestal to support the people who support me. What I know is that leaders must be dedicated to love and empathy to create the support for those who follow them. People don't like following those who won't sacrifice for them.

I firmly believe you need to embrace love and empathy as both a person and a leader to be happy. My intention is to always take care of those around me by giving, because I possess knowledge that can be of service to them. It's almost impossible for me to *not* help others. That comes from my love for my father. His suicide showed me how to hate, but it was my own attempt at suicide that showed me how to love him. The day I put a gun to my head was the day I truly understood the value of love and empathy. I began to renegotiate how I saw his choice. I know how easy it is to lose people. I know how hard life can be. Some people have no idea of the struggles that can come their way, but I do. I have been gifted this incredibly diverse life filled with difficult trials and painful stories, but I survived. I learned about the life-changing power of empathy. Dr. Brene Brown said, "Empathy is a choice, and it's a vulnerable choice because in order to connect with you, I have to connect with something within myself that knows that feeling."[11] Empathy changes lives because, as Dr. Brown asserts, it "fuels connection" (2013). Sympathy, conversely, "drives disconnection" (2013). According to Dr. Brown, empathy creates a reason to connect emotionally while sympathy keeps the emotion at arm's reach.

Connecting with people in need of empathy is highly rewarding. It is the reason I started writing. I began writing poetry and essays after my father died, because it allowed me to communicate my feelings. When I didn't have the words to explain to my mom how badly I felt, I would write a poem and show her. I would feel happy for a moment, even as she cried, knowing that I was at least being understood. My mom always maintained her empathy, so that she could help me through my dark times. Writing was my first step in developing the courage to express myself. I have written *Defy the Darkness* because I know someone will need to

---

[11] RSA, "The Power of Vulnerability – Brene Brown," 15 August 2013, (21:47), https://youtu.be/sXSjc-pbXk4

hear my story. Someone will transform because of what I've written. My story is a model for anyone who has felt self-destructive, anyone who doesn't think they belong, and for anyone who is just surviving.

I have enormous empathy for every person who is struggling on their own. They are likely gripped by the same fear that held me underwater for nineteen years and are afraid to speak about their emotions, their feelings, the hatred, or the pain of fear of judgment from people who have no understanding of the context of their lives. I respond on social media to anyone and everyone I possibly can with the singular hope of giving some young kid out there a little more time with his father. I want to give a father and mother more time with their son or daughter. I don't want to meet kids who have seen tragedies. If that means writing a book and giving it away, so be it. I want to stop the impossible, but empathy for the same pain I suffered will drive me until my last breath. Why? Because I love people and I don't expect a damn thing in return.

In fact, that drives me in many of my endeavors, including my marriage. I met my wife on a dating app called Bumble. I had made a pact with myself after my previous relationship to dive in and look for exactly who I wanted. I had two relationships that were driven by passion. They turned out to be relationships of unrealistic expectations and lack of communication. In the summer of 2016, I decided I would start my quest to find the woman who would be a true personality fit for me. I dated online for six months and was lucky enough to catch my wife at the right time. We matched and began an incredible journey that led to where we are today.

What makes this story so incredible is that had it been just one year earlier, I wouldn't have been ready. I knew what I wanted, but I needed to develop a clear picture of love that most importantly included what I needed to eliminate. What I decided I needed after everything I had been through was someone who was empathetic above all. I hate small talk; I always have. At some point, I learned to drive right past small talk and dive into people's souls. After the first time, I began to find what I truly loved. Empathy brought me immediate attraction. I would go on dates prior to meeting my wife and meet women who just didn't have what I was looking for within.

When I matched with my wife, Val, the connection was instant. Our texting was involved and flowed. I knew Val genuinely wanted to understand who I was and, more importantly, why. It is easy to ask someone who they are and what they do, but it takes skill to connect the dots and start asking the next questions. Val knew what she needed to ask for me to reveal my true nature, because she had been through it before. At twenty-seven, she knew what she was looking for just as much as I did. It didn't take us more than two days of texting before we set up our first date. I was in the best place I had ever been, and it showed.

I remember walking up to Val for the first time and feeling nervous excitement. It was rare for me to experience nerves, and she knew instantly; she smiled and hugged me. I'm certain she said something, but I was too distracted by her energetic beauty and my nerves to recognize what it was. All I recall from that moment was knowing she was the right one for me. I don't believe we get it right with the term, "Love at first sight." I believe it's an instinct similar to how I felt with my dad. I knew he was leaving, but I also knew Val was staying from the moment I hugged her. It was as if this comforting energy took hold and calmed my restless mind. Maybe it's more like, "Love at first feeling." I will never forget the feeling that descended on me. Even now, when I see her, no matter how long I've been gone or where I've come from, I feel at peace with Val.

She had picked out a place called Camp Bar for us to meet; little did she know I didn't drink. As we talked, she began to unveil my past without any prompting from me. She truly wanted to understand me and promoted my expression. It was uncomfortably rare for me to have that feeling around someone else. Her intuition brought out my darkness but also tamed its manifestation with empathy. She learned on our first date what I had gone through with my father, the beatings I got after him, the bullying in high school, the difficult things I saw in the military and afterward. I told myself, "I may as well tell her and let her decide if she can handle it." She loved listening to me and her empathy was a completely new interaction for me. She appreciated my honesty and applauded my strength. It wasn't the quiet uncertainty I was accustomed to; Val was as attracted to my honesty as I was to her empathy. We had found exactly what we needed in each other.

I didn't tell Val about my own path to suicide on our first date, however. I knew it wasn't the right time or place for me. It was still too close for me to reveal to someone so new. It didn't take long, though. Not more than two weeks later, we cried while we ate gyros in a Greek restaurant. I exposed my deepest fear to her, and she shared in my emotion. There is no greater moment than one in which two people come together, one to express and the other to empathize. Few moments in my life have felt more powerful than that one. I knew I loved Val the first night I met her, but I didn't realize the true depth of our connection until that day. She chose to feel without expecting me to take on her struggle. Because of that moment, she had me for life.

The most important thing Val has done for me was to understand my definition of love. We talked about our definitions and having no expectations of each other before we met. Val has followed throughout our relationship. She wants me to go do what I want to whether it was a hobby, self-care, or pursuing my passions. I give her the same respect. We both know these things because we listen to each other. I push her to enjoy girls' night, get a massage, or take a vacation, while she pushes me to enjoy my days at the range, the military, camping trips, and my business ventures. We respect each other's lives and we don't define our relationship with unspoken expectations. Honesty is what defines our relationship, even when it is uncomfortable. Honesty, however, with all the love and respect we have to give.

At the time of this writing, Val and I have been together for five years. Every day, I work to create for her the best environment I can. For three years of our relationship, she was grinding her way through graduate school while working a full-time job and managing to fit in two days a week at a demanding internship. If I had thrust expectations on her, I believe our relationship would have crumbled. Instead, I was flexible and empathetic as she always has been with me. But absolute empathy is impossible and unattainable. It is not possible to take on 100 percent of the context of another person's life. That does not negate the power of empathy, it simply limits the expectations you should have on what others can do for you. Let me define empathy for practical purposes. In my experience and humble opinion, empathy is listening to understand. I demonstrate empathy by observing and listening the same way Val has done for me. The only way to truly understand what others are struggling with is to gather an understanding of their perception of the reality they live within.

People can tell you their life story and still leave out millions of important details. I know Val, but I also am aware that there is a lot I don't know about her. It's impossible to know every detail of her entire life, especially from before we met. I don't know how it feels to have experienced what she has experienced and what she continues to go through. She is pulled in many directions and at times she struggles with her mental health. I don't always see that. There have been moments in our relationship where I needed to tone down my desire to help her because I knew there were things I hadn't yet learned or simply understood. Val refers to herself as someone with high functioning depression and anxiety. During graduate school, there were many moments she felt at her breaking point with so much on her plate between work, school, internships, and most importantly being a mom. She even sold her condo and bought our beautiful first house while I was deployed to Afghanistan. She is remarkable though I know it takes a toll on her at times. During one particular instance, in which she was having a breakdown due to immense pressure of balancing everything, I attempted to offer my wisdom. It was immediately met with resistance to what I thought could help her. I struggle with this at times. I make such deep connections with people that it hurts to watch them hurt. As she poured out her anger about what I had said to her, I began to see the error in my ways. I was looking to fix something I didn't fully understand rather than simply listen *to* understand.

You can't 'fix' people. You can only guide them to fix themselves or whatever their situation may be. You can replace 'fix' with words like 'save', 'help', or 'change' but the results are still the same. I was able to reflect back on myself when I was struggling with the same feelings. There was a reason I remained quiet for most of my life. People tried to fix me rather than understand me. It doesn't take much more than dropping your ego at times to realize that there is more that needs to be said before I see the full picture. At that moment, I stopped her and told her I wouldn't bring it up again, but I did so compassionately. I knew my ego was the problem and if it remained, that hurt I was feeling would become hers. She was taken aback by my response, but ultimately took it for what it was. I needed to change my perspective on how I looked at supporting people. That 'fight' taught me about empathy, and it taught me about ego. If you want to help others, you have to show them how to help themselves. You also need to decipher at times what is needed: do they want to be heard or do they want to be advised? Val reminded me that she's not always seeking my wisdom or needing help, sometimes she just needs to be heard.

As I share this story, Dr. Brown's wisdom resonates: "Rarely can a response make something better. What makes something better is connection."[12] I began to understand that Val is no different from me. For nineteen years of my life, I wasn't ready to talk about it. I was lucky enough to have incredible people in whom I could confide in when I was ready. It became clear that day with Val that I don't know what I don't know. That is

---

[12] RSA, "The Power of Vulnerability – Brené Brown," 15 August 2013, (21:47), https://youtu.be/sXSjc-pbXk4

the truth in every relationship or friendship. You don't truly know people. You may know what they are going through but you often don't truly know how it feels or the full details. This is why I find judgment simply not that useful. Why judge a person when you have no idea what choices they have faced or what limitations they have endured? I don't judge people; instead, I listen and observe. That is the best way to show your empathy. People speak without talking. It is the profound nature of empathy. Body language can tell you so much. Pay attention and learn to understand actions *and* words. I could have gotten upset at Val for not taking my ideas on board, but I would have been a hypocrite considering all the ideas I had disregarded throughout my own life. What she needed was connection.

These days, with Val being so busy, I am focused on empathy. I don't get upset when she forgets things because I forget just as much if not more. How can I judge her when I do the same? Instead, I find solutions. I work on ways to help her prevent herself from forgetting important things, taking as much stress from her and onto me as I can. She is working harder than I am, so I work harder for her. I don't expect her to do the same, but I know that because of what I have been doing for her, she will likely do the same for me when the time comes. I also don't expect her to return what I have given. My strength doesn't come from her supporting me; it comes from within myself. It isn't just Val who makes me happy, though she does bring an incredible amount of joy and connection to my life. I am responsible for my happiness. My understanding of life, my perspective on what is hard, and the empathy that I have developed is responsible for this long-lasting happiness. Sometimes you need to know how dark it can get to know how much you can take. My darkness has defined me in the best way possible because I have allowed it to become my inspiration.

I live with love and empathy in my heart, regardless of what I endure. Those who have wronged me don't descend into a resentful and hateful heart; they are upheld within me as moments I have learned from and as people who brought me to where I am. When you stop hating and start learning to love the dark moments in your life, you begin this deep transformative process within yourself. It starts with deep linguistic processing. How you internally talk to yourself creates your mindset for the day. Remember, consistent mindset creates perspective. If you learn to love yourself for who you are, in the long run your daily mindset will create a perspective based on self-love. Self-love requires sacrifice though. You must sacrifice the guilt, the shame, the jealousy, and the blame. Self-love is action with accountability. You must hold yourself accountable to your physical and cognitive actions.

Learning to eliminate the negativity helped me to overcome my self-loathing. I developed my process before I ever read Trevor Moawad _It Takes What It Takes_, but I wish this wisdom had been available to me when I was a kid. Moawad works with some of the finest competitors in the world; people such as Seattle Seahawks quarterback Russel Wilson, who won the Superbowl using Moawad's model. That model begins with eliminating negativity. What you consume is what you become. Moawad's process requires self-awareness but you have to understand that choice is an illusion. If you want to be a more successful person, you don't get to choose. You have to execute the habits and fundamentals that create success, not the habits that create mediocrity. This applies to anyone, from athletes to single parents. It isn't about being positive—it's about not being negative. Eliminate the choices that are getting in the way of your goal! I recommend Moawad's book, or any of the books I have referenced, because they will help you to cultivate your perspective.[13] Whether they are better or not, doesn't matter. What does matter is that learning is fundamental to whatever success you are seeking.

When you begin to love learning, especially about yourself, you start a journey that values the same knowledge spoken in different ways. *Defy the Darkness* is another way of discussing the same strategies Moawad uses; though he is likely to speak to athletes on a much deeper level. We are two voices spreading the message; that's the important part. Everyone learns differently and every style is important when it comes to spreading the message to people who understand different styles. Gary Vaynerchuk is the master of this idea. Speaking the same message using a thousand different styles is

---

[13] Moawad, *It Takes What It Takes*.

exactly what he purports people should do to succeed. Learning develops the ways in which you can describe your message, which will only enhance how it is spread. Ultimately, it always starts from within you. It will always be your message.

I had to begin to define who I wanted to be, which led me to personally define words like love, self-love, and empathy. To stand accountable, I needed to be able to understand exactly what they meant to me. This is important to do for yourself. It is easy to tell yourself you are going to be honest, but it's even easier to lie to yourself. That creates internal dissatisfaction with yourself. To truly love yourself, there needs to be accountability. Your dreams are only attainable if you have the vision to get there. Vision only works if nothing is blocking it. Your vision of who you want to be must be defined clearly enough to mirror the habits and behaviors you must emulate. Look beyond the obstacles, elevate yourself, and consider your life from a perspective that reaches beyond who you are now. Hiding your eyes and ears from the truth is not going to change a perspective of self-loathing. You must be willing to hear the hard truths about yourself. You must be willing to see your failures. Most importantly, you must be willing to *do* something about them rather than spiral into self-loathing.

Love yourself by demanding accountability, but don't expect perfection. Expectations will instigate insecurities, if you don't live up to them. Accountability is the idea of making the right choice to become who you want to be. If you don't make the right choice, don't dwell; eliminate the idea of choosing the wrong one again. When you stand against yourself and scrutinize choice, you learn to love who you become. Freedom, as important as it is for the nation, can be a very dangerous venture for individual mindsets. Fueling success, love, or empathy requires specific restrictions for behaviors to develop. For example, success and love require a rigorous work ethic, while empathy and love require listening. Success is no accident. It is instead a long path, riddled with effort and internal forgiveness. Guilt, shame, and regret have no business in success; they are the death of dreams.

It is love and empathy that stand as the fundamentals for success and happiness. You must love yourself and what you do to be successful at it and happy with it. You must be empathetic to master self-love for it is self-empathy that becomes fundamental. Empathy not only creates connections with others; it creates a connection between your past and future selves. You have undoubtedly made decisions in the past that you regret. It takes empathy to learn to respect the reasons why those choices became necessary and to love yourself regardless. Your dreams rely upon your ability to forgive yourself. Your mental health relies on your ability to love who you are and who you will become. Dare to validate yourself instead of looking for validation from others. Whatever you need to hear right now, let me be the one to tell you: You are incredible. You are worth it. You are enough. You are strong. You are beautiful. Love yourself—because no one else can do that for you. Love yourself.

Chapter 6

FREE YOURSELF FROM JUDGMENT

E very day when we wake up, we begin to think. Sometimes we think about what happened the day before or in the more distant past. Other days, we immediately start to think about what's happening right now or what will happen in the future. Often, however, it doesn't take long for judgmental thoughts to creep into our minds. It doesn't matter if you are the purveyor of judgment or the victim of it. For some, judgment is so familiar that there is no recognition that it's even a problem. To others, judgment is what they rely on to cope with their own situation. Judgment isn't an obsession or an addiction—it's a result. We live lives so entangled with negativity and judgment that it is incredibly difficult to find somewhere that it *doesn't* exist.

The media relies on judgments to incite fear-based reactions like anxiety and panic. It is sometimes legitimate, but most of the time is not. Since "If it bleeds, it leads" was popularized in the 1980s to describe the focus of the news cycle, not much has changed. Even now, social media has certainly ensured that "bleeding" stories stay relevant. Drama is always relevant, but that doesn't mean it is a good thing. This chapter will discuss why your energy should not be wasted on judging others or humoring those who judge you. I will focus on "shadow work" here: the neutral and positive self-talk you engage in daily within your mind that helps you grow and develop.

My shadow work began after my first deployment to Afghanistan. Three days after I came home, I tore my ACL while teaching a Brazilian jiu jitsu class. I loved teaching jiu jitsu. I wasn't the best practitioner, but I was the only one with a real background in the gym; that made me the guy. I taught for free because I loved it. The night I tore my ACL felt like it was going to be a good return to life. It was an opportunity to hang out with my best friend, Chris, who has always shared my passion for martial arts such as jiu jitsu and Muay Thai. As I started class, a new guy joined and I forgot to give him the normal script about not using leglocks. Well, our first drill, which focused on escaping and defending from guard, was when it happened. He was in my guard, stood up, grabbed my left ankle, then tucked it under his arm and fell back from his standing position. The momentum of his fall dislocated my knee and tore my ACL with a *pop* that made everyone in the gym stop and turn. In my mind, the world stopped.

There was no real physical pain, but I knew what that sound meant. It meant I was done. It meant I wouldn't be doing anything I wanted to do for a long time. It meant I might be kicked out of the Army for medical reasons. It meant that trying out for Special Forces was off the table. It meant the life I saw before me was no longer possible. My mind zoomed to every worst-case scenario. I sat back, somber and disassociated from what was happening around me. I didn't want to talk to anyone. I remember the guy who did it trying to apologize. My only response was a serious toned, "Back up, now."

I didn't blow up at him, but I wasn't kind about what had happened. I have never bothered addressing that man because it wouldn't do me any good. I was upset at the moment, but I was also collected enough to not say anything to him apart from communicating what I needed. I needed space, so that's what I asked for. Telling him he had ruined the next year of my life wouldn't have been true, nor would it have made me feel any better. Nowadays, I look at it like I stepped onto the mat, so I took the risk. I blame myself first because when I take responsibility, it offers me an easier path to think through and overcome. I don't have to waste my time wondering what he was thinking or why he did it; I just focus on evaluating what is in front of me, isolating what I can control, and acting and executing on what can be controlled.

Back then, in 2012, I wasn't where I am now mentally and emotionally. I was on active duty leave and was then sent to Fort Knox, Kentucky for reconstructive surgery and to recover. Being on active duty meant I had to be treated at a military facility. I became a part of the Warrior Transition Unit to repair and heal my broken body. Being dropped 500 miles from home after a rough deployment and a potentially career-ending injury meant I wasn't happy. In my mind, I was defeated. At that point in my life, my body was my ticket to living my best life. I felt like I was suffocating on the stagnation that had been forced upon me. I blamed the Army for making me go to Fort Knox and for all the suffering I went through there. Fort Knox was purgatory for all intents and purposes. I didn't quite know where things would end up but you knew I had to wait. My time at Fort Knox was the loneliest I have ever felt. It was where I began building my process of evaluation, isolation, and action, and it all started with understanding thoughts and words.

About two weeks into my time at Fort Knox, I was told I needed to attend a class. I chose a mindset class over another on finances. I don't remember the name of the instructor, but I remember him being a large black man with a calm voice. When he spoke, even though none of us wanted to be there, we all listened. That gentleman had an incredible presence and filled the room with a powerful energy. What he taught us would change my life, but only because I gave that knowledge the power it needed to grow. He gave us an understanding of how to utilize cognitive behavioral therapy to help ourselves.

Cognitive behavioral therapy is simply the idea that thoughts create feelings, feelings create behaviors, and behaviors reinforce thoughts. I believe this works if you commit to it. I used it to transform myself while also leveraging my strengths to overcome my weaknesses. I started by writing down a quote that really spoke to me while I was struggling alone in my room. It was a quote from *Batman Begins*, when Liam Neeson's character is explaining to Bruce Wayne how to become something incredible. This quote was what I captured on a piece of paper that I taped to my mirror in my single room: "If you make yourself more than just a man, if you devote yourself to an ideal, then you become something else entirely . . . legend."

After the class, I followed the instructor's advice and read that quote every single time I looked in the mirror. I internalized it nearly every hour of every day for eight months straight.

The truth is, Fort Knox was the loneliest time of my life. It was isolation before 2020 taught everyone what isolation really felt like. Imagine being stuck with only yourself 23 hours a day with limited ability to move and no friends or family within 500 miles. My deployment left me with a façade of external stability hiding a dark and disconnected internal chaos. My mind never stopped thinking which also meant I didn't sleep more than one hour a day. My wars, domestic and abroad, left me in a state of constant hyper arousal. I paid attention to everything every second I was awake. Any large bang would send me into a panic that I didn't allow others to catch onto for fear of judgment. Any military-aged male was a threat in my mind and crowds became a nightmare. Any piece of garbage or any broken dirt on the side of the highway could send my heart rate through the roof. I was suffering from PTSD but I was surrounded by men and women I believed deserved to be diagnosed with it more than I did. After all, I was just there to recover from my ACL tear. I didn't even hurt myself overseas. At least, that's what I told myself.

I began to realize that it was my own judgment of myself that was really brutalizing my mind. Blaming yourself first is important, but if you don't control the narrative then it will dominate you. That is the reason why I created my process within the context of telling *my story*. Evaluating the problem was never an issue for me. As I have said, isolation became the key to my transformation. When you focus on isolating what can be controlled and act accordingly, you become decisive. It is simple and immediate. You ask, "Can I control this?" If the answer is, "No . . . fuck it," you should move on to something you *can* control. If you fail to connect the successes, the failures become overpowering. It is the 'small victories' that make big differences.

It was around this time that I developed an attitude that I refer to as the "fuck it" mentality. I don't know exactly when it happened but relying on the "fuck it" mentality brought about a significant change within me. For most of my life, I was afraid of how others would judge me, my choices, or even the issues that I would think about. I didn't know if people would understand how much I loathed myself, and I certainly didn't want them to feel pity for me. I hated watching people sympathize because of my father's choice. I didn't want their apology or their pity. There was nothing I wanted from anyone. I was effectively isolating myself because I wished I would just die. Back then, I didn't want anyone to change that feeling. I was comfortable.

Fort Knox was a significant success for me. The sheer stubbornness and will to overcome something that I had personally seen others left the military for was nothing short of incredible. I physically and mentally beat myself into submission despite being alone. I had to learn to be my own support group. I had to learn to win when no one was watching. I had to have the integrity to take action for myself. I recognized the loneliness of that place and realized the only way out was overcoming. It became my only choice as I sacrificed every other option for the success of getting released back home.

When I returned from Afghanistan and after the seven months of rehabilitation for my ACL, I pushed into college life and returned to my National Guard unit. Over the next three years after my deployment, I would go on to tear my other ACL twice. I've overcome two ACL reconstructions. One on each knee and I still have a successful career in the military. I attribute my ability to keep going to my process of evaluation, isolation, and action. My first injury taught me how hard being unprepared to change can be. I promised myself I would become adaptable. My injuries taught me to trust my voice and to be empathetic to my own context.

It wasn't long after my knee surgeries and my first deployment when I began to unravel who I really was separate from my closest friends and family. I've always had a powerful way of connecting with others, but I rarely exposed the true depth of what I thought about on a daily basis. I reconnected with past friends and made new friends who showed me a new way of living. I was exposed to going out to bars and being around a lot of people who I didn't know. This was never my environment, because it was what led to my father's downfall. As a result, I never drank anything other than water and I always played to the crowd.

I would have just as much fun as the people I was with, but at some point, the question would always come: "Why don't you drink?" At first, I would be immediately turned off and would usually resort to internal frustration about being asked such a personal question. Other times, I would let it go and offer a simple answer like I had family issues with alcohol. I don't remember when it first happened, but I actually started telling people the truth. I believe I chose to tell someone who was just drunk enough for me to think, "I don't think they'll remember this, anyway." When I told them, my perspective began to change.

From that point on, I began to be more honest with people at bars. Being sober, I would simply answer the question with brutal honesty. The conversation would transition pretty sharply afterward.

"Why don't you drink?"

"My father was an alcoholic who committed suicide when I was six years old."

My response was clinical. The delivery was sharp. The typical reply would shift into an apology, but at that point I was already in "fuck it" mode and didn't care. When you've seen what I've seen, no response will ever make any real difference. Occasionally, though, people would throw me curve balls. Questions would follow, which was something I was not always prepared for. I would answer with as much honesty as I could allow myself. I never brought up my own thoughts on suicide, but I would tell people pretty much anything else I was asked. I was remarkably open for how closed off I really was. It was as if I was always waiting for the right person to see the breadcrumbs I was leaving. It made bar hopping an incredibly therapeutic experience for me. That is probably the last thing you would expect to hear from someone who has lived a lifetime of sobriety, but it is what it is. Everyone finds their way of overcoming in their own way. People were going to bars to drink away their problems, while I was going to expose mine.

The bar is where I began to really understand people. I was never one for judgment, so I didn't judge. I became curious. Those who talked to me often had very deep conversations with me about life. I felt like a therapist at times, as people would express very dark and concerning issues. I didn't feel any better than them; in fact, it was often the opposite. While they were offloading their problems, I was still dying from my own. Few would have guessed that I was vacillating between life and death every day of my life. Regardless, I listened to them and I helped. I learned that I could be a force for good, but I didn't practice what I preached, so I could never judge them.

At the end of the day, I don't judge others because I don't know the context of what they've been through. That is why I always listen first. You can't be 100 percent empathetic, because you can never know 100 percent of someone else's story. A person thinks 6,000 thoughts a day. That is over two million thoughts every year. Even one year of someone's life is nearly impossible to truly comprehend. There is darkness within everyone. We hide from others because we don't know how to share all of our feelings. The hesitation grows but still the idea of what others will say grips us with fear. It is rare to find someone who will listen without the intention of responding, yet finding it remains our hope. People want to be heard, not judged. It goes back to empathy. You must listen to understand and watch to pay attention.

You may find yourself on the other side, however. You will undoubtedly come under the scrutiny of judgment at some point in your life. What do you do? There are many types of judgment, from people judging the clothes we wear to the decisions we make, but there is only one way to overcome it all: trust yourself. If you listen to what everyone else is telling you, you will lose the most important thing you have: your voice. There is a reason I told the story about my ACL reconstructions at the beginning of this chapter. There was no judgment that came from that story, so what was it? It was the answer to trusting in your voice. (Reread it if you need to.)

Empowering your voice is the only way to truly overcome judgment. It isn't about shutting everyone else's voice out; it is about developing your trust in your voice above all others. You can listen to the judgment or completely ignore it, but things will slip through that catch you off guard in both scenarios. The only way to ensure that judgment doesn't run your life is to empower your voice to overpower whatever judgment comes your way. I listen to judgment and welcome it, but I always decipher it with my own voice. If I teach a class and everyone but one person loves it, I can't hang myself on that one person. I can take their judgment and feedback as a learning point to incorporate for the next time. My voice tells me I still bring value to the rest of the people. There is more to it than just trusting your voice, though.

Getting to the point of empowering your voice requires you to understand one simple fact of life: No one knows the context of your life; not your mom or dad, brother or sister, significant other, friends, or coworkers. No one has been there for 100 percent of your life. Only you have been there. Take that deep breath and say it: *Only I have been there for myself through it all.* You make your choices based on everything that has happened to you, and only you, in your life. You're going to mess things up and make mistakes because your context didn't equip you with everything you need. Here's a newsflash: No one ever gets it right. The world eats everyone up at some point and then spits them out with problems, some with more than others. You know most of yours; if you don't, well, keep reading.

If you have made it to this point, you are likely to have introspectively looked at your own mental processes and considered how to improve. If this book hasn't offered you clarity, don't worry: Life will be sure to offer it without your asking or approval. That's just how life works. You may not get to choose what happens, but you *do* get to choose how to react. Moments in your life will come and go. Memories will linger, some will haunt, and others will fade. You choose to give each moment and memory power by using your voice to empower it. When you empower a moment of failure or judgment, that moment becomes a self-fulfilling prophecy, whereas an empowered moment of success creates a foundation for more success.

Your context is yours to mold and shape, and isn't up to others to determine for you. I chose not to look at my ACL tear, which would later lead to tearing my other ACL twice, as a burden on my career or my life. It gave me an opportunity to slow down and develop my mind, which was something I had neglected to do for far too long. Three years in a row I tore an ACL, but I didn't give up. I didn't fall back into a depression. I evaluated what the problem was and how I had dealt with it before. I isolated what I could control, and I dominated my recovery through action and resolve. People told me that I should be out of the Army with injuries like I had suffered. I said, "Fuck that. I'm staying in." It was like Jordan Belfort's monologue in Wolf of Wall Street . . . "I'm not leaving. I'm not fucking leaving!"

I built my voice into the strongest noise in my head, not just through my problem-solving process but by eliminating and sacrificing things in my life. Just as Trevor Moawad asserts: "choice is an illusion."[14] If you want to have the strongest voice in your head, you have to be willing to cut out or silence whoever trumps your own. Strength comes from what you are willing to *not* do. If you have a family member that insults you and demeans you; stay away from them. If you follow social media influencers or groups that are negative and derogatory, unfollow them. If your toxic ex won't leave you alone, block them. It might require you to cut out your negative friends. You may need to leave a negative

---

[14] Moawad, *It Takes What It Takes*, 71.

work environment. You may need to address the fact that your parents, family, or friends don't support you in the ways you need. These are all hard conclusions to reach, but they are the choices that determine who you become.

You must escape the judgment of those who do not bring you value by either negotiating the relationship or leaving it altogether. Who you choose to listen to matters. When you make the decision of who to listen to in your life, keep a few questions in mind: Have they achieved the goals you wish to achieve for yourself? Are they where you wish to be mentally (whether that means happy or strong, or any other emotion you deem worthy)? Have they had to deal with a similar situation? Do they truly listen to you and understand you? These questions don't need to result in your cutting people out, but they do allow you to manage the hierarchy of voices that speak to you. Are there people in your life who you probably shouldn't be taking advice from? If there are, you may want to address that.

I just want to highlight this one more time before I close the chapter. Your family will undoubtedly be the biggest challenge for many of you. I am not insinuating that you have to cut off your family. I *am* saying you need to address this fact and make your own decision. You are allowed to love people who aren't there for you. You are allowed to let go of people who are toxic. You can move on from those who would rather hold you back for their own comfort. You are allowed to let relationships fade if they no longer know or understand you; or maybe they never did. Whether that's a family member, friend, or significant other, this is about expectations. Think back to what I shared earlier about not having expectations. Disappointment occurs when you expect others to change or to respond to you in a certain way. You have the choice of who is in your life, how they are in your life, and what is going to consume your energy. You are allowed to make these decisions! It's your life, not theirs. They may have good intentions, but that doesn't mean it's the right way for you.

Choose your voice. Choose yourself.

Chapter 7

LEARN FROM OTHERS

onfucius once said, "By three methods we may learn wisdom: First, by reflection, which is noblest; Second, by imitation, which is easiest; and third by experience, which is the bitterest." In this chapter, I want to discuss this quote's deep meaning and why learning is so vital to helping you become who you want to be. Learning develops and grows the brain, but above all learning is an undeniable investment. Knowledge cannot be taken away from you. It can only be minimized by the people around you and your surrounding environment. The truth is that everyone affects you. It is your choice *how* they affect you.

When you find yourself being affected deeply, where do you turn? Where do you turn when the trust and love you thought was there has eroded before your eyes? What do you do when the truth is finally revealed to you? Every person you meet will offer to you the full spectrum of emotions, if you give them enough time. Some will reach their extremes sooner than others, but at some point, everyone will hurt you. It is what you choose to do with that hurt that defines you. How you choose to mentally comprehend the situation is what will determine your personal growth and success. If you limit yourself to just what you are feeling, you have already lost. You must extend your thoughts beyond what you are feeling and grab ahold of your innate ability to learn the truth.

The truth is that if you want to grow your ability to learn, you must stop focusing on what actually happened. Instead, you must focus on how you learned, fundamentally, from what happened. The situation doesn't actually matter. Developing a path forward always outweighs full comprehension. Dwelling diminishes hope, and hope is a representation of what we think is possible for ourselves. Where does diminishing your possibilities leave your future? You will never fully understand every part of every situation. Some situations we simply don't have the capacity to understand. People die with the only truth that will ever matter. No amount of time, investigation, or dwelling will ever provide you with the answers you seek.

What I am trying to help you understand is that truth is not the end all, be all. The truth is always helpful, but it will still hurt; whether you know the truth, you will still feel the pain. What is so vital to this topic is a single idea: Taking stock of the situation and finding value in what happened is precisely what overcoming is all about. That is learning. (Read this sentence one more time, if you missed it.) Learning must be a search for value, if it is to be worthwhile. Going to school every day and hating it doesn't teach you a valuable lesson. Getting punched in the face by life teaches you a valuable lesson, because pain is attached to it. The pain is the value. The value found you. The faster you learn to take the first steps in search of value, the less pain you will suffer.

To truly begin, learning is a skill. If you don't begin to develop your skill, it will remain a difficult prospect. The defining proposition should be understanding what you are seeking. Your destination has requirements, and the outcome doesn't come without the process, work, and sacrifice, but above all the knowledge. Learning is the only way to get to where you want to go—and stay there. To stay there, you need to learn what to watch out for next. Evolution doesn't stop. The world doesn't slow down. If you want to maintain happiness, you have to continuously search for more of what makes you happy. Very few people are happy doing the same thing every day of their life.

All too often, you may find yourself in a place where you are temporarily happy. One good thing does not replace the fact that you don't know where you want to go or who you want to be. Learning requires you to trust that you can learn from everyone and everything you encounter. This is a difficult step. How do you learn from someone when you clearly have more experience than them? Or more schooling? Or more deployments? Or whom you outrank? The question of context comes into play as I answer these questions. No one has ever lived the same life as anyone else. Therefore, the knowledge derived is not always the knowledge you expect to find. You don't know what you don't know. Incredibly powerful information can be learned by observing or listening to or even feeling someone.

As children, we tend to learn by imitation. Watching our parents or siblings gives us an idea of what we are able to do. It is as simple as matching the behavior we see to what the mind and body can achieve. The idea of thinking is incredibly difficult to explain to someone who doesn't yet have a full grasp on language. Children watch and listen. As we grow, it seems that we lose the need to maintain that skill. It is almost as if watching and listening no longer provides us with the same rewards. We retain the skill in many ways, but we learn to apply it to only those things that interest us. That is why learning must be a search for value.

Somewhere along the way, we lose touch with the importance of learning. We become secure in the presumption that we don't need more knowledge or wisdom. Some are more likely than others to fall into this trap; arrogance overtakes their will and looms like a shadow over their relationships. There is a line between arrogance and confidence, but it is not a thin line:

arrogance requires no one else. Confidence is the idea that you have the right solution. Confidence has nothing to do with believing you are better than anyone else. Confidence is knowing that you are equipped, and the importance of learning is to equip yourself for what is to come. It is not to live without others.

I can assure you that when you watch and listen to people without judgment, you open your eyes to a deeper skill. The ability to watch, listen, or feel objectively as something happens and derive value from it can profoundly change the way you learn. It isn't about how you see others; it becomes a way to see what they do, say, or express as options for molding yourself. Equip yourself by watching, listening, and feeling your way through every person you encounter. Pay attention to people who fail—and learn from their mistakes. Watch those who are maintaining—and observe the success that keeps them where they are and the failures that hold them back. Above all, pay attention to those who succeed, for they have equipped themselves with the knowledge, habits, and perspectives responsible for that success.

What I have witnessed in successful people is a passion for learning. These people *need* to learn more. It isn't that others inspire them; what they learn from others is what has inspired them. The context of one person's life doesn't always transfer easily to another's. Being able to relate and reflect on what we see, hear, and feel is where transcendence begins. This is a two-way street. We must perceive the story as having some semblance of relatability. Conversely, we must possess the self-awareness to use reflection. The introspective deep dive, as I say, is necessary to understand what knowledge you might need to equip yourself with.

It isn't easy to learn on your own, to reflect using your sole knowledge. This is what I focused on for almost twenty years. My pride and my fear of criticism is what nearly led to my downfall. I would struggle within myself and reflect on situations for days, weeks, months, and years after they had occurred. I would often fail to recognize the fundamental truths attached to many of those situations. I would find myself dwelling on the things I could not change. Don't waste your life struggling! If you are struggling, dwelling, or overanalyzing, you are not equipped with the knowledge you need to overcome. Reflection works best when you add new perspectives into the mix. It isn't comparison; it is evolving what works best for you and equipping your mind with the right response to the situation.

It is challenging to discuss reflection without referring to what I believe is the most important way to learn: experience. I questioned whether to tell you that you should try to avoid making my mistakes. The truth is that my mistakes brought me here, to writing *Defy the Darkness*. I made the mistake of wanting to kill myself. As much as I needed the experience, I didn't need reflection to tell me it was wrong. The moment I put the gun to my head, I knew I had learned something; I just needed some time and someone else's perspective to understand what it was. The experience made the difference. Losing my father made the difference. Being beaten by a man whom I didn't trust made the difference. Being bullied made the difference. War made the difference. There are so many experiences that taught me lessons. Reflection brought me clarity, but the experience forced me out of my comfort zone.

I can't tell you to avoid making mistakes. In fact, I might tell you to go and make mistakes because doing so will teach you something. I wouldn't be the man I am today without my failures and mistakes. But more importantly, I wouldn't be who I am without the powerful events that have broken me. It's what I have learned from the most emotional moments that has made me realize how strong I am in this game called life. I didn't become a warrior when I joined the military. I was fighting long before then. War was simple for me, because I had fought all my life. I am comfortable in the chaos now because every day was chaos. I was learning so much as I continued to fight; I just didn't know it. The struggle wasn't clear, but the experience forged me into a survivor and a warrior.

I have always been an introvert. I suffered on my own because it felt comfortable to do so. The problem is that if you are not gathering different perspectives or gaining additional knowledge about what you are struggling with, you get nowhere fast. Your life revolves around a cycle of internal distress. You don't change if you cannot look outside your own box. It is incredibly easy for people to live their lives in a bubble or echo chamber. You follow a routine of cyclic thoughts and unhealthy habits, because it is comfortable. You may never realize the mental and physical toll it takes on you. Your comfort will defy what is necessary for the growth and success you seek.

It is the quest for knowledge that will bring you closer to what you require to grow: people. Our societies were not built by men and women who isolated themselves within their own minds. I know how hard it can be to take that step beyond yourself. I've stood on the knife-edge wondering which way I would fall. To be honest, I was lucky to fall where I did. A light breeze could have left these pages and words unseen by you. A single moment could have changed the course of my history and therefore yours. I fell forward into the arms of those who would consider with me how to find the value I didn't see. Many times, I heard the message yet it wasn't clear. It wasn't clear until I began the quest to learn. Only then did the message hit its mark. I could not see what I could not decipher.

People are the translators of their own knowledge. They help us see the foundation of strength that our minds have been built upon. Learn to trust that everyone will affect you and therefore, can affect you. Seek and you will find. Ask and you will be answered. Understand, however, that what you seek will not always be what you actually find. What you ask will not always be answered in the ways you expect. If you knew the answer you were seeking, you wouldn't have asked the question. Part of the journey is not knowing where you are going. Learn to accept that you don't know every answer. Find humility in the fact that some experiences have eluded you. Find humility in the idea that someone else may unlock the answers you seek within yourself.

Step outside yourself. Defy the comfortable feeling of isolation. Take a step toward your goals by reaching out to someone for knowledge. Don't place an expectation on the answers. Be humble enough to know that the answers you seek will not come without the journey. Your path requires initiative. It requires you to have the courage to go and find what you are looking for, although you must also know that you may find something else. Wisdom isn't about knowing the right answer. It is about knowing what is right in front of you.

To build something, you must know how. To build something you don't know how to build, you must learn. To learn, you must know why. Is your *why* powerful enough to make you learn something you don't want to learn? I didn't know how to overcome all the terrible things that happened to me. There weren't many role models with similar experiences, so I didn't pick just one. I chose them all. I chose to watch and learn from every person I could. At first, I had to learn how to simply define where I wanted to go. I had to defy death. Learning to defy the darkness taught me how to survive. Defining how to survive gave me the confidence to fight. And when the moment came, when the battle hung in the balance, I won. Not everyone wins the battle, which is why I choose to learn from others.

All I want is to give someone else the chance I wouldn't give myself. It is what drives me, and has required me to learn as much as I can. I had to delve into parts of myself I dared not go near for nineteen years. Like a monster, I kept it locked away. I dared not tame it, because I didn't understand it. Then, all at once, I fell into my *why*. I saw how dark it can get. I lost myself in the darkness for a moment that nearly ended my life. To recognize what I felt that day was a terrifying experience. No one should ever have to fall that far and have to decide between life and death. I wrote this book to help you understand how important it is for you to take the first step toward expression. Learn from everyone you can and trust that they will have an impact on you.

Learn who you are by recognizing your reflection in others. You will find people you love because they share a piece of you. Search for the pieces of your puzzle by searching for those who complete you. As you experience this world, find value in what you remember and in what you feel. If you can't find value, you haven't found the moment that will reveal it to you. Be patient. It *will* come. The more you search, the easier it will be for you to find clarity. And when you face your demons, remember this:

Defy until you can survive.
Survive until you can fight.
Fight until you *win*.

Chapter 8

CHOOSE TO LIVE

"It's the moment when humanity is overcome by majesty
When grace is ushered in for good and
all the scars are understood
When mercy takes its rightful place, and
all these questions fade away
When out of the weakness we must bow
And hear You say 'It's over now'.
I'm alive..."
—MercyMe

How do you write the most important chapter of your life? This book began with the idea to help others overcome what took me nearly twenty years. I was at war with myself for a long time before I found it within myself to choose to live my life. Moments brought me to my knees; I would beg for the strength to get through what my own mind was doing to me. I never realized that I could only blame one person for ravaging my mind with the pain brought upon me throughout the years: myself. That person is me. I chose to hurt myself. I chose to define myself as a victim of the choices of others. What took my twenty years to realize was simply this: Hell is within you.

I didn't understand the simple fact that I was in control of myself. When I cried, it was because I wanted to. When I was angry, it was because anger is what I wanted to feel. I chose to feel every bit of pain I could, because I believed it would bring me closer to my father. It was my choice to live through hell. When I fell to my knees, mourning for a man who wasn't coming back, it was my choice. Sometimes, thinking about it now, it seems simplistic to suggest it is a choice to feel. That is correct and yet it's also wrong. It's that simple, but to make it that simple requires complex emotional training. My life trained me to be who I am now. Every ounce of pain I felt brought me to the level of strength I now possess.

This chapter is the rawest version of myself that I will ever be. I thought about, pondered, or flat out wanted to die every day for nineteen years—from the day my father killed himself to the day I put that gun to my own head. I hated the sight of people enjoying their lives with their dads. I hated seeing commercials that had anything to do with parenting. I didn't even tell anyone the story about my last memories of my father before he died until well into adulthood. I suffered alone, in silence.

I hoped that one day, someone would look inside me to understand the storm that raged.

I remained hopeful throughout my life until the day came when no hope remained. It took me nineteen years to drain every ounce of hope from my soul. I had seen enough adversity for several lifetimes. I was done. I remember barely holding it together in a sociology class at UW-Whitewater after a rough break-up a couple of weeks prior. I held myself together until I found my car in the parking lot. Then, I climbed inside and fell apart. I sobbed. I didn't even know why; I just let go. I fell to questions such as: *Why is this happening to me? What did I do? Why am I here? Why am I still here? Why should I even stay?*

Every question loomed closer to the real answer I longed for. I longed for an ending to the nightmare. I wanted to stop hurting people. I wanted to stop hiding. I wanted death. I wanted my father. As I drove home, in the worst state possible, I attempted to answer those questions. As I drove an answer home for each one, I just traveled mentally deeper into the territory I told myself at eight years old I would never go near. That drive home felt like an eternity, although it didn't take a half-hour. Every minute of the way, I poured out my soul for the people I was hurting. I was diving into parts of myself that I had long been scared to explore.

Every feeling hit me in the heart like a dagger. Everything I hated about myself was released as I spoke. My voice was decimating every ounce of hope I had for a future. The suffering was relentless. Crying and stumbling as I walked inside the house, I fell into the fires of my own hell. I chose to succumb to my darkness and live within it for that moment. I dropped to my knees and searched for the answers. I was lucky that I didn't find the answer in my hand that day. I was lucky that day didn't result in another man being taken before his time, another man who possessed all the potential in the world. You know the rest of this story. I'm still here. I didn't choose to die that day. I chose to live.

What brought me out of that moment was the shadow work I had started in Fort Knox. I had been preparing for this moment. My own voice was ultimately my greatest demon and that day became my greatest savior. I had been falling for nineteen years, but that moment brought me clarity. Every moment that had come before had equipped me to evolve and adapt. The people who I surrounded myself with were mentally placed where they needed to be. I unconsciously retained the people who supported me, and I expelled the people who were responsible for drama or pain. My thoughts had slowly begun to change after Fort Knox. With the principles I developed, I continued to fall back on my stubbornness. I refused to die that day, because none of what I was saying was true.

I took a good hard look at the shame, regret, and guilt I was still carrying. This chapter is basically Judgment 2.0, but it delves far deeper than in Chapter 5. If you want to know the recipe for a lifetime of struggle, mix together any of those three feelings. Shame, regret, and guilt are the most powerful thoughts in your mind, and they will deceive you into behaving in every detrimental way possible. Each has its own nuances, but they are all equally nondiscriminatory. The effects on our actions speak loudly. I have seen much of the same behavior that I showed because of these in hundreds of other people. Gary Vaynerchuk describes them as "poison" for good reason. I see them as the terrible trinity. They will dominate the landscape of your life, if you don't address them; that is the purpose of this chapter.

I was ashamed of my father for a long time. Kids who deal with a parental suicide are more likely to commit suicide themselves. I was ashamed of my father for choosing suicide, because so many people had told me it was a selfish act. I listened because I was too young to understand what it really meant. The shame I felt for my father had transitioned into how I looked at myself. I wasn't who I wanted to be, and I couldn't live up to what I thought my father would be proud of. I struggled with my self-worth, because I didn't know where to place my value. I was giving my value to a man who was dead. Some of you are giving your value to people who continue to prove to you that they don't deserve it. Don't forget where your value belongs: within you. You determine your worth by how you speak to yourself. Find your problem, evaluate it, isolate the things you can control, and act upon your solution.

The guilt and regret of what happened between my father and I was a far more complex story to navigate.

With shame, I was able to connect the problem to miseducation. I knew I needed to take a step back and develop an understanding of myself separate from my father. I regretted letting my father leave that day, because I knew he wouldn't be coming home. That was more than just an idea; it was a deep, emotional connection to the moment. It was my own action that failed to stop something I knew would happen. I felt every second of it, and I continued to feel it for a long time thereafter. How you deal with situations like suicide, trauma, assault, or anything else that leaves a deep emotional connection to the moment requires an ability for you to renegotiate the story itself.

I did a lot of unconscious, or unknowing, renegotiation throughout my childhood. What brought me a clearer understanding of this renegotiation was my recovery at Fort Knox. The isolation forced me into a deeply introspective state of mind. As I began to overcome my depression, I renegotiated how I viewed my injury. I was able to create strength out of what I had initially thought was my weakest moment. I began to recognize my ability to do the same with anything I struggled with mentally. The important factor was how I retold the story. This is what I began to consider. This is what initiated my research into people who have not only overcome adversity but who also become iconic and successful. The most successful people are likely to share a few important habits. Chief among them is the fact that they turn their difficult and troubling moments into moments they overcame, survived, or learned from. They confront their most difficult moments head-on.

In the summer of 2015, after I had nearly given up on life, I had to create a process to change the nineteen years of damage I had caused myself. I had a shattered foundation and an unclear idea of who I wanted to become. I did have information, however: I knew who I *didn't* want to be. I didn't want to be involved with alcohol, drugs, or tobacco. I didn't want to commit suicide. I knew I had an incredible work ethic, but that I was lacking direction. I also understood the weaknesses that had brought me to my lowest point. My story still had power over who I believed I was. As I began to redefine myself, as I have shared, I did something that I had never done before: I began to expose my vulnerable thoughts of suicide to my closest family and friends, which became fundamental in my transformation.

The courage to reach out offered me a chance to perceive my thoughts through other people's perspectives. This wasn't necessarily a foreign concept to me, as I had done so at so many bars during my college life, but I gradually began to cross-pollinate ideas. I started to apply the knowledge I had gained from overcoming in my life, while also researching and listening to people who had grown from their own experiences of adversity. To build my process, I started the same way I started back in Fort Knox. I stopped focusing on the negative. I simultaneously developed a list of books, podcasts, YouTube videos, social media influencers, and people in my personal life to whom I gravitated as a result of their positive impact.

I began to consume content that reminded me of my own greatness. I still remember watching Les Brown's speech on YouTube: "It's Possible (Les Brown's Greatest Hits)."[15] Brown's words resonated with me as I began to mend my damage. I focused on what worked. I knew that putting words into my consciousness every day and repeating them helped me. With that in mind, I watched Les Brown's video at least twice a day for around a year. Not to mention the myriad other videos from legends such as Tony Robbins, Eric Thomas, and Gary Vaynerchuk that I consumed.

I created my environment by sacrificing the world around me. I worked on schoolwork, worked out, or drove while listening to those videos on repeat. Every day I would literally cry as I listened to the words. They offered me something unbelievable: the idea that my life might actually be worth something. Every word spoken by those incredible individuals brought me one step closer to developing a voice within myself that would become unstoppable. To get there, I would put in hours of shadow work, every day sewing up the shredded pieces of my heart. Eric Thomas would hit me hard by saying, "When you want to succeed as bad as you want to breathe, then you'll be successful."[16]

---

[15] Les Brown, "IT'S POSSIBLE (Les Brown's Greatest Hits), 10 May 2014, (59:56), https://youtu.be/gXuSMjrx_e8

[16] From "The Secrets to Success" by Eric Thomas.

I was surrounding myself with the strongest mental coaches on the planet every minute that I could—wake up and listen; eat breakfast and listen; drive to school or work and listen; finish class or work and listen; work out and listen. I spent these hours listening to words of positivity while focusing on holding myself back from reverting to self-loathing. I spent a year really working on myself and realized that my self-talk was strong, but it was mostly negative. I had been listening to my voice, but I didn't have the voice necessary to foster my growth before my suicide attempt. I wouldn't allow myself to love who I was. My transformation became focused on cutting off my thinking and listening to the words that constantly promoted optimism and strength.

Putting in the mental work became a part of my long-term transformation, but it worked because I created the best environment I could over time. It all goes back to the fundamentals. I took a step forward by choice. I started to pull my strengths together from other parts of my life and planted them like the seeds of the great oak trees behind my home. My empathy for others was unrelenting, and I took steps to offer it to myself. I created forgiveness within myself for myself. Repurposing the integrity I learned from the military was forcing me to do the right thing for myself and not just for others. Integrity drove me to build honesty within myself. My character began to reform, as I developed within the environment and the experiences in which I had immersed myself.

It hurt every day to struggle with internal thoughts that shifted between wanting me to hate myself and hearing the fact that I could be great. I cried and I sobbed. Even as everything I consumed told me I was better than where I felt I was, I suffered. I was creating the vision I wanted for myself in just wanting to be happy, but I realized that being happy meant creating the strength to be happy in any moment and not just in the good times. It meant wrestling the power from moments and injecting that power into my mind and my voice. I had to expose to myself that it didn't matter who was to blame or why I was the way I was—the only thing that mattered was what I was going to do about it.

Producing happiness cannot start with negative thought. It begins by looking at every situation in a way that can bring you value. Value is found in everything. The essentials that allow us to survive each day bring us value. Air provides the oxygen we need to breathe. Food and water sustain our bodies and provide us with energy. Shelter and clothing allow us to maintain our core temperature. Your mind is its own ecosystem, and value is still king at its core. Providing value to yourself is paramount. Self-esteem is the air for your mind. Words and thoughts are the food and water. Our environment and the people within it are the shelter and clothing that protect us. The holy trinity of environment, words and thoughts, and self-esteem are what determines our own internal sense of value.

My environment was a burden on me for a long time; it was something I had no control over. Eventually, however, my environment began to change, while my thoughts and self-esteem continued to kill me. It was my ability to analyze that helped me understand what I needed yet burdened my mind. Putting your brain into hyperdrive is physically and mentally stressful. As you continuously stress your mind and body, you create habits and cycles that begin to affect all aspects of your life. The flow of habitual living begins to define thoughts and feelings. Learning to interrupt your habits allows you to understand where the stress originates. Your environment is often a major contributor to your mindset. Surround yourself with negative people and watch yourself become negative.

Engineering my friendships was probably one of my greatest strengths as a kid. I was happy being alone, so the few friends I was willing to make were those whom I trusted. It was never about a lack of choice; I wanted to be alone. That comfort of being alone kept me from compromising my beneficial environment. I was lucky enough to know what it was like to have a bad human in my life. I was even more fortunate to have been strong enough to make the decision to be willing to live a life of loneliness rather than force myself to have bad relationships and friendships. The obvious downside of those decisions led me down the path to suicide, but it also saved me. My friendships and relationships were deeply rooted connections. Had they been weaker, I would have been weaker. Had some of them not existed, there is a much higher probability that this book wouldn't exist along with my life.

Writing *Defy the Darkness* required me to understand how my environment shifted over time. I began at a time in my life when I was growing exponentially, when I helped a friend build a business for himself. The positive and growth-focused nature of our endeavor inspired me to work even harder for myself. This book has been in my head for twenty years, but it required the right environment and people within it to inspire the words. No sooner had I gained momentum, though, than I was faced with the opposite end of the environment spectrum in 2019, when I deployed to Afghanistan for nine months. The cramped and poorly structured environment stifled my creativity and ambition, which limited my focus. When I returned, I found myself free to create the environment I needed to find my rhythm once again.

Returning to normal life, I was able to choose whom I allowed into my life. Then with the outbreak of COVID-19, I was forced into isolation with just my family. Unlike my time at Fort Knox, I was at home in isolation. My preparation over the prior five years had allowed me to return to simple, yet trusted tactics. I cut out the negative. I reminded myself how I got there and how I had survived. I found myself and my passion in the silence and the light tapping of my fingers on the keyboard. I loved watching my story develop, knowing that I was selfishly going to help someone with my words. I reminded myself that I didn't just love it: I needed it. Every minute I waited to finish meant one more person might end their life. I couldn't allow another little boy to grow up without his father. Not if I had a chance to reach through that darkness. I had to work, or I wasn't going to be happy with myself.

Throughout the time I spent developing this book, my words and thoughts rarely demanded alteration. My vision and the goal remained so firmly planted in my head that it really only met resistance when other things required my focus. Finding a flow came naturally, but at the expense of my emotions. Writing this book has been heavy. Many of the memories are incredibly powerful, and some are still quite raw. The strain on my emotional energy still hit me hard as I wrote these chapters. A piece of my soul flowed into these pages as I expressed my heart in ways I never have before. Writing has always been my path to expression. I am able to speak but writing offers me the time to perfect the art of word choice. Writing defines the evolution of my mind, because I very much *feel* my way through it.

The power I gain from reminding myself of my own words and thoughts drives my actions. I begin to realize the value of what I have done, what I have said, and what I have lived through. There are moments in my life that will never repeat themselves. Times that I will never forget. Days that brought me to my knees. But in every moment that I have lived, my mind has not abandoned me; even in my times of need. Words have played the greatest role in my survival: words that no one will ever hear like I have heard. The words inside my head and the thoughts that changed my life did so because I gave them the power they deserved. I gave those simple words the power to change my mind and my life. They are the words that built my self-esteem.

For almost two decades I felt inadequate. Was it unreasonable and irrational? Absolutely. What is rational sometimes doesn't make a damn bit of difference, though, does it? Perspective is your reality. Inadequacy is an incredibly debilitating feeling and a burden on your self-esteem. You are the words you say, the thoughts within your mind, and the environment in which you interact. Each gives you a straightforward understanding of your self-esteem. Confidence does not come from materialism. Happiness doesn't come from a big wedding and an attractive partner. The corner office or the dream job doesn't make you the best person in the company. What creates happiness is your ability to remain grateful for who you are and placing value in the story of you.

Your vision of your past determines whether you feel shame or guilt or regret about it. What have you left on the table? Do you hate your failures? Or have you created an understanding of how those failures brought you where you are today? If you think the same way you've always thought, you will never learn to change. Redefining your life, your choices, and your feelings is necessary to learn, feel, and act differently. The deep feelings of shame must be addressed. Guilt and regret have to be confronted. The longer you hide, the more your body will suffer. The more you will suffer.

I am attempting to speak directly into the depths of your soul. You have been holding back for too long. You have wanted to tell someone your secrets for too long. You've listened for what seems like a lifetime and have waited for the right person to come along and change you. Sometimes, each minute that goes by brings those thoughts of failure, of shame, of regret, of guilt bubbling up in the fore of your mind. You are distracted by those thoughts that make you feel you are no longer present. Your world is a fog because your thoughts shroud the hope you once had. You feel like you've tried everything. You feel like you're going to break down. You're scared that someone else might see your weakness. You're scared that someone might ask you the one question you fear. You feel like you're losing control. Losing your grip on "being strong." You feel done.

You are not done. As long as you have been alive, you have fought for yourself. You are a warrior in the trenches of the greatest battle you will ever fight. That darkness you've been facing wants you to lose. You are the light that breaks through the darkness. You are not weak for breaking down. You are not weak for losing your grip. You are not fearful for not wanting people to ask you the question. You are not crazy for feeling distracted, or cloudy, or foggy. You are not a failure for the shame, for the guilt, for the regret. You are not a bad person because of one, or two, or more choices gone wrong. You are human. You are allowed to make mistakes. You are allowed to fail. You are allowed to feel something. You are allowed to fall to your knees and ask why this is happening to you.

But you are also allowed to love yourself. You don't look for the greatness in yourself because you have surrounded your thoughts with the ones that are the most painful. You have strength; it is why you are still here. Fighting your war has brought you to this point. It has immersed in these words. Your battle has made you reach out to these words I am saying to you. That is strength. You *want* to live. You want to find the best within you, or you would not be here. These words are no longer mine; they are now yours. You must choose to give them power. You must choose to have the courage to believe in something else. Not the negative thoughts, but those that exist here right now. You are strong. You are powerful. You are not inadequate; you are just unequipped. You are loved. You are capable of loving yourself. You are amazing. It's okay to feel. It is okay to cry, to break down, to let go. Emotion is power. Believe in your power. Trust your emotion. Choose to say no to the pain, the anger, and the need to hate yourself. Forgive yourself. *Forgive yourself.*

Choose to defy the darkness.
Choose to love yourself.
Choose empathy.
Choose forgiveness.
Choose to live.

Chapter 9

SPEAK YOUR TRUTH

When I finished the first draft of *Defy the Darkness*, I knew something was missing. This chapter almost didn't make its way into the book because it required something of me I had never done before. It required me to tell my story to the world and not just to those around me. I began taking this idea seriously when I started to build my social media following on platforms such as Tik Tok, Instagram, YouTube, and Facebook. I watched others make a difference daily in the lives of millions, all the while knowing I had a story that could do the same. This chapter is a part of my journey that required a new perspective, one shrouded with uncomfortable feelings. This chapter required that I speak my truth.

My life has been filled with trials, tragedy, and triumph. In many respects, I have been historically silent about most of it. In fact, "suffer in silence" was one of my mottos for longer than I care to admit. I learned from my father, from the military, and from society that silence was mandatory; staying silent was easier than facing the darkness. It isn't convenient for people to deal with my mental health, so *I remained silent for them*. If there is one thing I have learned from becoming a social-media influencer, it's this: There are a lot of people out there suffering in silence. The fear that manifests itself in our silence destroys the *power of you.*

I know this because it began within me. I unknowingly observed my father remain silent for the six years I saw him alive. Imitation is the strongest form of learning, in my humble opinion. We often fail to recognize the consequences of what we imitate; that is, until they take us down the wrong path. My father may have been the best actor I have ever watched. His secretive thoughts taught me how to hide—not how to survive. I've also always been a good actor, which is why people didn't know the full extent of my internal battle. I spent those nineteen years exhibiting a façade that was slowly crumbling. The destructive habits and thoughts simmered within me like a volcano ready to explode. My father was the first of many to teach me that lesson.

When I imploded, it was due to my own choice. I suffered in the same way my father did because it was what I knew. I learned that much from him, even if I didn't learn to share in his resolve for self-destruction. What connected me to my father more than anything wasn't some premonition; rather, it was the moment we diverged. We had walked down similar paths, but when the fork came, as Robert Frost wrote, "I took the one less traveled by, and that has made all the difference."

The Road Not Taken

Two roads diverged in a yellow wood,
And sorry I could not travel both
And be one traveler, long I stood
And looked down one as far as I could
To where it bent in the undergrowth;

Then took the other, as just as fair,
And having perhaps the better claim,
Because it was grassy and wanted wear;
Though as for that the passing there
Had worn them really about the same,

And both that morning equally lay
In leaves no step had trodden black.
Oh, I kept the first for another day!
Yet knowing how way leads on to way,
I doubted if I should ever come back.

I shall be telling this with a sigh
Somewhere ages and ages hence:

Two roads diverged in a wood, and I—
I took the one less traveled by,
And that has made all the difference.

~Robert Frost~

This chapter is about the road I did take: the road of expression. Expression has served as the undercurrent of this book but hasn't been the highlight until now. This chapter required me to fulfill my purpose before I could write it. This book required me to see my old self in the people I help every day. It required me to step onto social media platforms like Tik Tok and Instagram (@ dylan_sessler) and speak my truth. I had to talk about my life unapologetically to shed the fear that ignorance had placed upon me.

I didn't begin expressing and speaking my truth for myself. I had been quite secure with myself at this point for a couple of years. I began expressing and speaking my truth because I knew I could help people. I started making Tik Tok videos about mental health in April of 2020, not long after Covid-19 took the world by storm. I reached 300,000 followers in a matter of months, and grew a following that communicates with me every single day to tell me that I am the reason they chose life. My story helps people around the world. My words, my wisdom, my perspective are what drive people toward change. I don't mention this out of arrogance; I mention this because it punched me in the face when I realized what had happened.

I built something I never had the privilege of experiencing. People followed my voice and my words. I expressed myself daily on Instagram and Tik Tok just to help one more person. What I did, one person at a time, was help. I responded to comments and direct messages all day long. I made emotional videos that resonated in the hearts of those who were suffering. Some of you who read this book will still remember the very video that inspired you to follow me. For that, I am more than honored; I am thoroughly grateful. The simple reason I am grateful for your following me is that you have given me a sense of purpose I've always known I was built for.

I'm grateful for the pain, the struggle, the violence, the tragedy, the self-destruction—all of it. I needed to be just one millimeter from pulling that trigger to help all of you. I needed to lose my father to be in the here and the now for you. I had to hold onto the tattered shreds of that darkness to choose life. My life's pain and tragic turns inured me to the supreme value of expression. I see it so easily now. I see the pain behind people's eyes, in ways that still sometimes surprise me. I think it always will. The power my gift requires is the humility of what I almost did to myself.

I almost ended the most beautiful thing I could offer this world. That is the most profound statement you will ever make to yourself, if you have ever stared down the barrel of a gun, held a knife or razor in your hand, looked into the emptiness of a pill bottle, felt the call to rip the steering wheel in a way no one would understand, or felt the coarseness of a rope. To each of us: We know our way out. I've stood on the precipice of death, just like you. I had to choose for myself, much like you probably have. I almost didn't survive because I chose to fight alone. My father didn't survive because he chose to fight alone. There are few times where I tell people to not follow my actions, but this is one of those times. Don't fight alone.

I saw the necessity of expression all my life, but it was never validated by someone who had faced it like I did. I've never found anyone with a story like mine; the truth is, I probably won't. To be honest, I never needed it. I needed to not feel alone throughout it. I wanted the validation that someone could survive it. I just couldn't see that it *was* a possibility. I couldn't see the path ahead of me because everything just felt so dark. I wanted to be told I had more to give. I wanted to be told that my life was necessary. I wanted to just let it all out, so someone else could understand what to do with it all. I wanted to be taught how to overcome it.

I was getting in my own way by remaining silent and always hiding behind the fear of judgment. I was hiding behind my own ignorance. Rather than trust in what I needed to do for myself, I chose to distrust the abilities of others to listen to my story without reacting judgmentally. I would not allow others within the heart of my darkness. I simply didn't believe anyone else could handle what I would tell them. I didn't trust those around me to know how to help me. I was afraid of what would happen if I released the floodgates of my story. I couldn't risk pushing that evil on others when I knew I could keep holding it back.

Remaining silent taught me that I loved others more than I loved myself. My decision to hold onto the very things I knew would eventually kill me was easy. I was internally honest with myself, but I lied to everyone who asked me the simple question, "How are you?" To this day, that question means more to me than most will ever know. I personally ask that question, not in passing, but with meaning and authority. I am able to determine with most people whether they are lying to me. I know because I was the best at answering that question without people ever realizing I was struggling.

If you watch someone long enough, they will *show* you how they are feeling. If you get the opportunity to watch and listen as they talk about themselves, they will show you everything you need to see. People can't hide their unhappiness when they speak, even if they think they are good at it. Their own ignorance, much like mine, is often an invisible façade in the eyes of those who have been there. When I speak to people, I disarm them within minutes whereas it could take hours, days, and years with a therapist. I am a "wrecking ball of perspective," as one of my clients once told me. My vision cuts through those metaphorical walls, as if they are a house of cards.

I have spent my life building myself up to become the person I needed when I was growing up. Now as a Life Coach and Motivational Speaker I ask people to express their demons, and I guide them through their personal darkness. I believe if my father knew the current version of me, I could have helped him save himself. My father has remained my inspiration. His choice is what inspired me to write this book. Much like my goal of being the person I needed while I was growing up, I wrote this book for him. This book is the perspective needed to come out alive.

You can't fight your battles alone and be held prisoner by the fear that keeps you from speaking. Someday, you're going to realize that you're tired of not doing more for yourself. Maybe you've already been there or are currently finding that place. If you have arrived at that moment, make the change. Find a person empathetic enough to simply listen to understand. Stop trying to be the strong one. You can't be the strong one when you're falling apart. Let go of the charade and get to the reality: You are not weak for expressing yourself. You are incredibly strong for having faced and survived it all.

What is necessary is a change in how you perceive your decisions. This was the intentional undertone of *Defy the Darkness*, but if it wasn't blatantly obvious to you, here it is: You need to see how other people look at your decisions. The best way to do this is with someone who is empathetic enough to understand that you had to make choices to ensure your own survival. I don't recommend throwing your story out on social media if you are not ready for negative feedback. You are human. You need to find someone who understands and can empathize. Someone who can help you see that forgiveness is necessary if you are to overcome. Not everyone is good at that part. This is the goal of therapy, but not everyone can step into the situations that you may be facing. Search for the right person or people.

If you struggle with expressing yourself verbally, try writing. Write about what you have faced, then read this composition to yourself. Your goal is to rewrite what you've written in a way that paints you as the hero, even if the hero has to just survive some parts. Write, speak, and rewrite your story. Continue to develop your story to support habits of self-love and self-care. This process takes years and can push people into very emotional states. I highly recommend you cultivate a stable environment, especially when you start addressing deep-seated traumas. I also highly recommend having someone who can guide you through the darker parts of your story. Someone with a high emotional intelligence and well-developed empathy.

The defining characteristic of my community is openness. People do not hold back when they begin to realize that I understand. Every day after my battle with suicide ended, I found my conversations with others becoming deeper. We were built to communicate. We were built to express ourselves. Our emotions are a testament to that fact. It is emotion that allows us to communicate on higher levels. We are stronger within the context of unity when we have the guiding principles of honesty and openness; it means we are using the full arsenal of human emotion. Additionally, it is replicated in the strongest teams and societies, regardless of race, creed, culture, etc. Honesty drives change.

Change is hard. It is hard to be honest and hard to change. It requires perspective. Change is fueled by empathy and is hampered by fear. Empathy and fear exist on opposite ends of the spectrum. Empathy and fear are contrasting mindsets, and I believe everyone will find themselves experiencing both at some point. What I come across most often is the fear of expression. This particular fear may have been learned from parents who simply were not taught how to express *themselves*. It could have been learned from being the product of an environment of silence. The fear is often produced by rational events or, in my case, from being too young to understand how to explain. For example, an abusive parent will often make their children feel guilty for having feelings, which then makes expression feel wrong to the child. The problem is that expression *feels* better when offered in a setting that is devoid of judgment.

When the knowing and the feeling are different, the silence becomes necessary for survival. Yet, it also feels wrong. The silence persists beyond this environment, particularly when it begins in the formative years of childhood. Good people grow into their adult lives and fear what telling their story might inflict on others. Therefore, people continue to carry the weight of their stories. They hold onto the pain, the suffering, and the struggle as if it will either hurt them or hurt those who will listen. To those of us who have overcome, we now recognize this isn't rational. To those who haven't yet overcome, the difference between rational and irrational often has no clearly defined line.

There are often two things that stand in the way of progress when it comes to overcoming and speaking up: Defining and Connotation. These are entwined but also lead to separate issues related to telling your story. When I speak about defining, I am referring to the concept of defining key words and how they fit into life. On these pages, you have already seen me do this with love, empathy, judgment, etc. Connotation, on the other hand, is a different beast. Connotations are the subjective additions we add to words. What are your "trigger" words? That is connotation. Both defining and connotation are important because they manage the very foundation of human interaction and communication: words.

If your intent is to change, you must speak your truth . . . but that is just the beginning. What I haven't shared with you is that you need to evaluate your story because it likely has definitions and connotations that don't mesh with your ultimate goal. If you want to become someone else, you must create the habits, mindsets, and perspectives that are in contrast to your present self. That begins with evaluating the words you use and how you use them. The meaning behind every word is incredibly important. If you are not good with words, learn to be good with words. They matter more than your TV, your car, or your money. Self-worth, self-respect, self-confidence, and especially, self-empathy come from words.

To properly evaluate your words, you *must* remove the emotion from the moment. Clear and calm thinking within a quiet space is often what I require. The next requirement is to understand the words you are using. I start with definitions. I read the actual dictionary definitions of words such as empathy, love, and kindness, but I don't stop there. I step out of the hardened definition that dictionaries provide and capture the malleable, human answer. I read books, articles, and opinion pieces on these words to capture a clear picture of how others define them. Research is *necessary*. If you don't step outside your own mental box, your singular definition will hinder your progress.

Definitions are simple. It's the constant maintenance and accountability that is difficult. In some ways, you must empower that definition every single day. In the long run, you need purpose. Why are you doing it all? You may have to sit with that question because the definition is king. What is the definition of you? If you had to put yourself in the dictionary, how would you write your own definition? What would you say about yourself? Would it be bad or good? What words would you use to show the world who you are? These questions have profound answers and elicit even more profound responses from the people you tell. More often than not, the definitions of ourselves don't live up to our true selves.

If I could leave you with one thing from *Defy the Darkness*, it would be the message of this chapter: Express yourself and learn from how you tell your story.

The following is one of the most common comments I get from my social-media followers who are struggling: "I always felt like others were worse off than myself, so I don't share what I go through. I don't want to bother anyone else with my own issues." If you find yourself comparing your story to other people's, you are destroying the only opportunity you have to change your life. You must express your story for no one else but yourself. It is not about trying to find someone you can beat over the head using your story. It was never about competition. It's about letting out the darkness that has been consuming you. Turning what happened to you into words allows you to rationalize. You create logic. When you speak to others, you begin to add better words and subtract destructive pieces. To become and maintain who we want to be, our minds require structure. If words are the skeleton of the house, definitions and connotations are the nails and glue that hold it together.

Understand that when you tell your story, emotion becomes necessary; but evaluating requires calm. William Shakespeare wrote, in *Hamlet*, "Cry, 'Havoc!' And let slip the dogs of war."[17] This statement literally and widely means to cause violence. For me, however, I view it as the permission to release the emotions and demons of the past. Release the violence, the abuse, the neglect, the guilt, the regret, the shame—let slip the dogs of war. They are not yours to contain. The people who harmed you are the ones who deserve that guilt. The ones who

---

[17] From *Hamlet, Prince of Denmark by William Shakespeare*

neglected you deserve to hold that regret. The people who hurt you deserve the shame. It was Anne Lamott who said, "You own everything that has happened to you. Tell your stories. If people wanted you to write warmly about them, they should have behaved better." [18] If you are the one who hurt or neglected people, remember you are still worthy of redemption; it begins within you. Who you were is not who you will be!

Don't fight this battle alone. Connect with people who will inspire you to hold yourself accountable. Sometimes, like me, it is nice to know that someone else knows—and understands. My mother checked on me, but my independence pushed me to overcome without her help. She, too, knew this was what I needed. I also showed the initiative to change, whereas, I never had before. My mother recognized that and allowed me the space to do what I do. When I have a purpose, I am Thor's hammer; I will persevere no matter what. I don't know how to give up when I find a purpose. I believe I am no different from most people; the difficult part is finding a purpose.

Finding your purpose begins with accepting yourself. I can't guarantee you will find the purpose you anticipate, but someday you will find something that drives you to fight for more. Fighting yourself detracts from you finding your purpose. The mental energy required to do both is very hard to manage and is why you don't see

---

[18] From *Bird by Bird: Some instructions on writing and life* by Anne Lamott

passionate people falling apart too often. Notice I didn't say "powerful" people. I said "passionate" people. Passion and power are two very different mindsets. Passion is what drives purpose and requires expression. Power is dominant and controlling, which drives people into isolation. Don't overpower yourself; be empathetic with yourself.

Find the *perspective* within the problem. Connect the *habits* to the perspective and build a mindset, daily, that's worth holding onto. It's the little things that make the difference. It's expressing that you're having a hard time with a good friend, who shows you the fault in your habits. It's the everyday maintenance you conduct to push yourself to heal. It's the first day of the rest of your life, and it matters more than yesterday. You matter. Your story matters. If to no one else, it *must* matter to *you*. You will never know what lays in your path unless you LIVE it. Now is the time to forgive yourself for what you once saw as necessary to survive.

Express yourself for yourself.

Chapter 10

CULTIVATE LEADERSHIP

have devoted my life to people. I have spent years of my life educating myself on how people learn, how they develop, and especially how they suffer. These are categories that help understand how to lead others. With that being said, leading people will always benefit from the perspective you gain from leading yourself. Leading yourself through your battles lays the foundation for empathy. In my opinion, empathy is the most powerful thing in our world. It is the foundation of good families, good organizations, good laws, and so much more. Great leadership stands upon the bedrock of empathy.

I want to share a story that hit close to home not long after I 'thought' I finished this book and it has everything to do with leadership and empathy. It was January of 2021 and I was finishing up the first drill date of the year with the Army National Guard. Right before we started up the bus to return to the armory, a soldier came on the bus to tell me something. He informed me that we would be having a short formation regarding the suicide of another soldier from our battalion that happened that morning. Four suicides in fifteen months since our deployment to Afghanistan turned some heads in our battalion.

News like that hits like a brick when you know suicide as intimately as I do. By January of 2021, I had just about 350,000 followers on Tik Tok but I couldn't reach the men that needed it most. It puts things into perspective when you lose. Numbers don't mean a damn thing if people can't hear you. There was a moment after that soldier walked off the bus that I had to face a choice. I had an opportunity to express what those four men probably never had the chance to hear... my perspective. I had spent the past year sharing my story on Tik Tok but this was the first time I was able to make an impact on people without a screen between us.

To be perfectly honest, it also scared the hell out of me to speak in that environment. As I've said before, the infantry and the military in general are incredibly tough environments. These are hard men and women who have been taught to show their enemies and their allies no weaknesses and no emotions. How do you step into an environment designed to teach soldiers to suffer in silence and share a perspective so deep and vulnerable? Let me tell you how from experience. It took an intense amount of courage, poise, and trust that I was still speaking to human beings. And, quite frankly, the message was more important than my reputation.

I simply began with the facts. Four men had chosen to end their lives in the past fifteen months. I began slowly and intensely. These soldiers had never met me before that day and they were about to learn how deep I was willing to go to get this message across. I knew that to reach into the hearts of these men, I was going to have to show them something I had never done in front of a group of soldiers. I was going to have to share my own relationship with suicide. It's easy to share yourself through a screen and on a podcast but I don't think that truly prepares you to watch the faces of people listening to your most intimate struggle.

I asked the question, "Where does suicide come from?"

A few responses came in like "depression" and "survivor's guilt," but they didn't satisfy me. I looked into the eyes locked on me in that cold bus as spoke with a heavy tone, "suicide isn't the problem, it's the result." I continued:

> It's the result of a lifetime of pain, suffering, self-doubt, bad parenting, lack of empathy, hate, hurt, lack of expression, loss, PTSD, trauma, bullying, disconnection, and so many more. It's a

result of being taught to suffer in silence rather than openly address the issues that destroy human beings. It's a result of being hurt and not being taught how to deal with that hurt. It's a result of leadership not listening to the actions of people just as intently as they listen to words. It's a result of not being able to communicate pain without the fear of judgment. Suicide isn't the problem, it's the result.

I could see the nods of agreement and the connection grew. I could feel these soldiers seeing a perspective no leader had ever discussed with them before. I gathered my courage for the next part.

I began to talk about my father's suicide. I told them what it was like as a six-year-old to watch my father lie to me for the last time. I shared the intimate detail of knowing he was never coming back and what it was like to comprehend that at such a young age. I wasn't speaking for me. This wasn't therapeutic for me. It was hard and emotional. It was terrifying in some ways but I knew so deeply in my core that it was necessary to show these young men an example of what suicide truly is and what it does. I continued on despite my fear.

I pushed further and further into my story. I spoke of the self-doubt, the self-hate, and the self-destruction that would regularly dominate my life after my father's death. Every story flowed into the next with each of them beginning to see what I really meant when I said the words, "Suicide is not the problem, it's the result." I wasn't regurgitating the Army's simplistic PowerPoints that we all have to sit through every year. I was hitting them in the gut with what it really looks like to be in that dark place.

As I came to the relatable part of my story for these soldiers, I found myself feeling a deep sense of preparedness. I slowed down for a moment as I spoke of my deployment to Afghanistan in 2012. I detailed the hardest things I saw; the American casualty that lost three limbs before finally dying, the Afghan who was missing half of his skull and still walking, the many Afghans who lost arms and legs to IEDs that were carried off MEDEVAC helicopters. These things impacted me in ways I could not have prepared for and I didn't hold back the emotion that began showing itself in my voice.

My voice and tone began to change as I choked back the tears. It's hard to hold back the emotions when you describe an American hero who paid the ultimate sacrifice. SSG Christopher Brown left behind a beautiful family; a wife, children, and a newborn who will always struggle when they think of him. That hits close to home to a man who knows how difficult it is to grow up without a father. I make it a point to share his story when I can because his death taught me to rethink my perspective on life. No matter how hard it feels, men like him must be remembered. That is exactly the picture I painted for the men who listened intently on a cold bus in Wisconsin one Tuesday afternoon in January.

As I was painting this story for them, I dug deeper into a part of me I had not shared in front of a group of people before. I shared my own path to suicide. It wasn't a moment of weakness; it was a protracted fall over nineteen years of struggle. My father's choice became an infection of the mind not because of him but because of me. I explained my rendezvous with guilt, shame, regret, and jealousy after feeling like I wasn't good enough after my father died. I expressed how hard it was to see a father and son playing catch when I never even had the chance. I poured out the dark thoughts of regret that I couldn't stop him from ending it all. Speaking the truth comes with a fine print. If you're not willing to accept that other people will judge your choices, you're not ready to speak and you're not ready to lead.

Telling those men that I had put a gun to my head six years ago was hard, without a doubt. What is even harder is losing one of them to suicide. I'd rather be judged by people that don't understand my choice than lose someone that is facing their own. I've embraced my story and with that truth, I've embraced vulnerability. I also remain dedicated to the strength needed for the infantry. Strength is both silence and expression. It is not one or the other because every situation requires something different. When facing down the enemy after being shot and shattered, silence might save your life. When facing down yourself, having the courage to express yourself to someone who can help might be what saves your life. That day, I led those men in a way they had never seen before. It wasn't about gallantry and valor; it was about connection and empathy.

The bond of brotherhood has always been strong in my line of work but that bond also comes with unspoken limits. When you're in, you're in but when you're out, you're out. It's not much different from most workplaces but ours carries a pretty hefty price for failure. The infantry comes with the expectation that you uphold the standards or you could risk the lives of your brothers. If you don't uphold the standard then you don't remain part of the in-crowd. If you're not a part of the in-crowd then you are relegated to an experience that is increasingly isolating.

We discussed this in depth because it is one of the biggest issues that cause people to turn towards choices like suicide. The script often plays out in a way that people who commit suicide are said to have isolated themselves. Is that really the truth though? What if they are trained to react in such ways by the myriad of people who push them out for being different, weak, or ineffective? With that being said, suicide prevention in the military is focused around talking about suicide which isn't the actual problem. Suicide is a plausible solution for people that are pushed away to the point of feeling worthless or devalued. The reality is that people can be harsh and when you've never been taught to deal with harshness, humans find creative ways to solve their problems.

Leadership is the real solution. Not the valiant and glorious aspects of leadership like leading men into battle or earning medals. I'm talking about the hard stuff. I'm talking about sitting down and listening to people even if we don't get along with them or they aren't effective in their role. Empathy requires listening to understand. Solving problems requires understanding the problems that eventually result in suicide. Men don't talk about their problems because no one shows them their voice or that their story matters. If you're struggling with suicide, it's quite likely that you've never been afforded the opportunity to tell your life story to someone who would listen without judgment. Talking about suicide can work but talking about why you think choosing suicide is even more important.

That is just the beginning. It can't just be limited to finding those who are in a vulnerable position but also those peers that make a difference. I forced men to talk about an issue that is highly prevalent to our gender, not just our job. I led the discussion because that is what leaders do. Leaders sit down and have hard talks. They show people it's okay to be human; to express. Leaders step out in front and take the emotional hit before everyone else. Leaders must also step into the line of fire for those who need to be defended. Far too many times I have seen soldiers pushed away from the unit for having issues rather than be mentored and incorporated into the unit.

Leaders must begin to look at prioritizing people over the three M's: mission, metrics, and money. I once had a soldier that struggled to maintain his fitness when he joined my squad. I was a younger man with a bit of a harder edge and I recognized instantly that he was going to have a hard time keeping up. The squad tried to carry him along but ultimately, one by one, they each left him behind socially. His performance continued to wane and eventually he began to show up late. I knew there was more to the situation because I could see the want to be a part of the squad but something deep down, held him back.

He didn't expose anything until it was far too late to truly help him and even if he had, he was facing a battle few could manage. His mother's drug addiction put him in such a place that he became the unofficial guardian to her children. She degraded and berated him constantly and consistently. He was in a broken home and the one thing that had taught him to trust again was falling apart before his eyes. Some members of the squad were incredibly callous towards him until I stepped in and changed their perspective on the matter. I showed them a different way of managing and supporting him rather than delivering the very same treatment he received at home. This soldier eventually failed two Army Physical Fitness Tests which carried the price of a general discharge. After his first failure, I was given the option to give him up to headquarters where he surely had no chance and no support.

Needless to say, I kept him because I only trusted myself to do the right thing for him. I chose the hard route. I met with him consistently during drill to discuss his fitness but even more importantly, his life. We talked about perspective, habits, and thoughts. We dug into the hard conversations and brought the hard truths to the forefront. It wasn't convenient and it didn't make the change necessary to keep him in the army. But it did have an impact, one that would take years for me to finally realize. He contacted me two to three years after he left the army behind to tell me that he had been in a very dark place and it was what I said to him that kept him going.

If I hadn't put in the work, would he have been another statistic? I like to think he would have found his way regardless but what if that was all it took? Maybe it was just one person showing effort to help him in his life. We meet thousands of people in the course of our lives. What if it simply takes one good person to remind us of our value? Let's change the world one person at a time. Whenever you finally see yourself through your battles, I challenge you to give someone a fighting chance at winning their own. Whether that is sharing this book with them, sharing your time and energy, or even sharing your story like I have shared mine, do something. I think that's called leading by example.

I call it leading with empathy. You don't have to be the leader that gets perfect results but what if you became the leader that helps others get the best results they can?

What if you were the reason that pushes people to see the best in themselves? That is a beautiful thing. That would bring meaningful value to both your life and the lives of others. There will be those who disagree with your style and your strategy but that's life. You'll never get everyone to agree but you can allow them the opportunity to speak and that, from my experience, builds respect.

You have an opportunity ahead of you but to build your value in others, you must allow yourself to see your own. Leading others will always benefit from you leading yourself first. Look within yourself and force yourself to love your journey even if it doesn't feel right. Stop trusting the feelings that have kept you in this dark place. I'm not anymore of a hero than you can be. You may even be better! I'm just a man telling a story. I am just as human as you, flesh, bones, and blood. What truly defines us is what we do with what we have. People may be known for what they have but they didn't earn it for no reason.

You cannot learn to overcome overnight. You can't heal from trauma or pain in a moment. That's not how life works. You may never let go of the memories of the hard times. Healing has nothing to do with forgetting. Overcoming has nothing to do with hiding. It has everything to do with leading yourself through the storm and looking at what you've been through with an empathetic perspective.

You will make mistakes. You will fail. You will hurt people. You will make bad decisions. No human being on the planet lives a perfect life to the point they don't face those moments. It will happen. Stop leading yourself with thoughts that don't match the reality of life. You're trying to be a perfect person in an imperfect world and you're surprised it isn't working. You want to give up?

Give up the bullshit act of trying to be perfect. Give up the lie that your mind is trying to feed you. Your body is telling you every day that your thoughts are unsustainable. They are killing you day by day. Give up on idealism and live in the reality that life is messy, painful, and tragic. When you accept the truth that life is not meant to be perfect, you become more forgiving of the choices you've had to make to survive. When you become more forgiving of yourself, it becomes easier to become more forgiving of others.

We all need a little more forgiveness in our lives. We all need to see the world through a more realistic lens; one that incorporates long-term growth rather than impossible overnight transformations. You want to change your life? Make a five-year plan and a ten-year plan because it will take a long time to rebuild ten, twenty, thirty years of self-destruction, if not more. You know yourself best. You may not like what you see but that doesn't matter anymore. It's easy to hate yourself. Dare to be different. Dare to spite that hateful person within you and find something you can love every single day.

No one else can lead you to your best self better than you can. Stop waiting. You're not alone in this. I didn't grow so quickly on social media because you're the only one struggling. I have been there along with millions of others. We are humans and we will suffer throughout our lives. Even I will suffer again someday. I will lose but you can be certain of one thing: I will never give up on myself so long as I have breath in my lungs. Even as I write these words, the feelings of how deeply I love life are so overwhelming.

For twenty years I hated life because I didn't understand it. I didn't even try. I wanted to hate life because it was easier to choose death. It was easier to believe there was no good that could come of my life. As you read this book, you see a legacy that could have never existed. If this book has impacted you then I hope you begin to look at your future differently. You don't know what is waiting around the corner. I didn't know that only five years later I would be helping save lives by sharing my story. I could never have known either. You're not a fortune teller but you are a warrior. Stop trying to predict the battle and start fighting so hard there is no other outcome but victory. Go forth and fight your battle like losing isn't an option anymore but do so with the perspective that makes that possible.

CONCLUSION

This book has been in my head for over twenty years. I knew at some point in my life I would need to write down what I have seen. I didn't have a clue what that would look like when I was younger, but I tried to remember everything I could because I knew at some point my story would be written. Maybe it was the power of my writing, or the understanding that I would need to build a legacy to overcome my father, but something just flat out told me, "You need to write this down someday."

I can still recall the notebook page that became my outline. I was sitting in a sociology class at University of Wisconsin-Whitewater, struggling internally and feeling that I needed to cry. Instead of crying, I focused on writing down what I wanted to cry about—my past. From that moment forward, *Defy the Darkness* became attainable. Little by little, I took steps to build my outline, reconnect with my old writing, and read books within the same genre. This goal was driven by something deep inside me that needed to come out.

My will to live was fighting for the air beyond myself that it needed to grow. The oxygen I needed was expression. When it comes to mental health, I would equate expression to the very air we breathe. When you are put into an environment that stifles your ability to express the true version of yourself, you suffocate. I have seen this in my own life and also in many others. This book was the reason, both metaphorically and somewhat literally, I started breathing. These are the words I wished for all my life.

All I ever wanted was someone to have been through what I had endured, so I could feel understood. There was no model for me to follow, so I stopped looking for a single model and learned the most valuable lesson I can now pay forward. Listen to everyone. I gave every voice the respect deserved. I took every word and dissected what it meant, and I made my own decisions. The only voice I ever allowed to be more powerful than my own was the voice I gave my father after he died. Realistically, it was always my voice. What has allowed me to find happiness was understanding that no one else's voice carries more power than my own. What made me consistently happy was learning that I needed to express who I am and not hide it.

If you are not understood, find a different way to explain yourself or someone new to talk to. Whatever you do, do not hold back. The hardest moments in my life came directly from holding back what I was afraid to discuss openly. Honesty creates accountability. Accountability creates change. If you hide the worst parts of yourself, you will likely remain the same and continue to live with the regret of not changing. No matter whatever emotion or adversity you have been trying to overcome and continue to face, find a place to express it. Whether it is sadness, anger, numbness, shame, guilt, or regret, let the emotion of that pain and suffering flow from you like water from a glass. Let it go. Defy the darkness you have faced for all these years, because there is more planned for you.

I hope this book offered you a glimpse of what is possible. I sought to show you that you have the strength to move past your struggle. That won't ever change. You might have flown to the highest highs or may be spiraling to your lowest lows, but you are still alive. Every breath you take is another moment of strength. Let the air you breathe empower you with the audacity to believe in yourself for one more day. Have the courage tomorrow to believe it again. Then believe it again the next day and the next day and the day after that. Keep believing it, even when someone tells you otherwise.

You have more to give, my friend. The pain and the struggle that has torn your life apart can destroy you or it can build you. It is time for you to build on the foundations of strength you already possess. You are complete. You are no longer lost. You have everything you need within you. You are not inadequate. Being ill-equipped does not make you worthless; it makes you open to knowledge. Being ill-equipped means, you have the potential for growth. Now is the time to change how you see your life and your story, like I have changed how I see mine.

I want you to write down your story so that you can detach yourself from it for a moment. Read it to yourself and learn where you can find value. See the strength that you have shown and, if necessary, rewrite it to depict for yourself how you grew from it. Your value as a person is directly related to how you talk about yourself and your story. Do what I have done—don't just read the words I have written. Take action for yourself. Don't just read this book. Make a difference in where you go from here.

My final words are to wish you all the best I can offer. Show kindness and empathy, because that is what people remember when they look back for good people. It is your choice to grow. It is your choice to place your life in your hands. Don't give up on it when you are so close to finding your path. Morris Mandel said, "The darkest hour has only sixty minutes." Keep going. Don't quit now. Defy the darkness within until you can survive. Survive until you can fight. Fight until you can win. Win by finding balance with who you had to be and who you want to become. Tomorrow only comes by surviving today.

Never quit on yourself.
~Dylan

#DylanSessler
#DefyTheDarkness
#NoOneFightsAlone
#IAmAVoice
#InvictusNation
#InvictusTribe

NOTES

Bassham, L. (2011). *With Winning in Mind*. Mental Management Systems, USA.

Brown, B. (2018). *Dare to Lead: Brave Work, Tough Conversations, Whole Hearts*. New York: Random House.

"Empathy." (2021). Lexico.com. Online. <https://www.lexico.com/definition/empathy>. Accessed 4 January 2021.

Glasser, W., Meagher, J., & HarperCollins (Firm). (2014). *Choice theory: A new psychology of personal freedom*. New York: HarperCollins.

Johns Hopkins Medicine. *Children Who Lose a Parent to Suicide More Likely to Die the Same Way*. 21 April 2010. <https://www.hopkinsmedicine.org/news/media/releases/children_who_lose_a_parent_to_suicide_more_likely_to_die_the_same_way#:~:text=In%20the%20United%20States%2C%20each,to%20suicide%2C%20the%20researchers%20estimate.>

Lamott, A. (1994). *Bird by bird: some instructions on writing and life*. New York: Pantheon Books.

Levine, P. A. (1997). *Waking the Tiger: Healing Trauma.* Berkeley, Calif: North Atlantic Books.

Moawad, T. (2020). *It Takes What It Takes: How to Think Neutrally and Gain Control of Your Life.* New York, NY: HarperOne.

Shakespeare, W. (2016). *Hamlet, prince of Denmark.* B. Mowat & P. Werstine (Eds.). https://www.folgerdigitaltexts.org/html/Ham.html#line-1.3.0 (Original work published 1599).

Thomas, E. (2011). *The Secrets to Success.* Spirit Reign Publishing.

Van der Kolk, B. A. (2014). *The Body Keeps the Score: Brain, Mind, and Body in the Healing of Trauma.* Viking.

Watkins, A. (2015). *Coherence: The Secret Science of Brilliant Leadership.* London: KoganPage.

Willink, J., & Babin, L. (2018). *Extreme ownership: How U.S. Navy SEALs lead and win.* Sydney, N.S.W.: Macmillan.

ABOUT THE AUTHOR

Dylan Sessler is a mental health advocate and coach who has spent years overcoming his personal hardships including being a survivor of parental suicide, PTSD, suicidal ideation, depression, and anxiety. He now spends every day helping and inspiring others to overcome their battles, see their value, enhance their mental health, and thrive via his mental health coaching business and various social media platforms.

Dylan is a U.S. Army Infantry veteran of 13 years with 2 deployments to Afghanistan and is a Certified Suicide Intervention Specialist through the Army's ACE-SI program. Dylan has public speaking experience, a podcast, and offers a group coaching program called **Pain Perspective Purpose Power** that is specifically designed for those who have a desire to heal themselves on their own. Dylan resides in Wisconsin with his family.

You can find out more at www.DylanSessler.com or follow his social media accounts @Dylan_Sessler to keep up with his newest developments.

Made in the USA
Monee, IL
30 July 2021